PELICAN BOOKS

A 43

INTRODUCING SHAKESPEARE

G. B. HARRISON

INTRODUCING
SHAKESPEARE

G. B. HARRISON

PENGUIN BOOKS

Penguin Books Ltd, Harmondsworth, Middlesex

U.S.A.: Penguin Books Inc., 3300 Clipper Mill Road, Baltimore 11, Md

AUSTRALIA: Penguin Books Pty Ltd, 762 Whitehorse Road,
Mitcham, Victoria

—

First published 1939
Reprinted 1941, 1948
Revised Edition 1954
Reprinted 1957

Made and printed in Great Britain
by Hunt, Barnard & Co, Ltd
London and Aylesbury

Contents

PREFACE 9

I. THE LEGEND OF SHAKESPEARE 11

II. MATERIALS FOR THE LIFE OF SHAKESPEARE 23

III. THE MODERN APPROACH TO SHAKESPEARE 46

IV. SHAKESPEARE'S COMPANY 69

V. THE ELIZABETHAN PLAYHOUSE 86

VI. THE SHAKESPEARE CANON 108

VII. DEVELOPMENT OF SHAKE-SPEARE'S STYLE 117

VIII. EDITING SHAKESPEARE 147

A SHORT READING LIST 172

List of Illustrations

PLATES

William Shakespeare: From the Engraving in the
First Folio   Facing page   64

The Hall of the Middle Temple   Facing page   96

IN THE TEXT

The Swan Theatre: A Sketch made in 1596   87

The Courtyard of the New Inn at Gloucester   88

The Exterior of the Globe Playhouse, from
Visscher's View of London, 1616   94

The Globe Theatre: Wood-engraving by R. J.
Beedham after a reconstruction by Dr J. C.
Adams   96

Preface

THIS book is intended for the use mainly of the general reader who wants to know something about Shakespeare and what modern scholars and critics are doing, partly also as a general introduction to the Penguin Shakespeares. For this reason I have used the text of the Penguin Shakespeares for quotation from such plays as have already appeared in that series. As the text of the Penguin Shakespeares differs in many ways from the older text, I have added a more personal chapter on *Editing Shakespeare*, to explain and, I hope, to justify its method. A brief list of books recommended for the serious student is added on page 172.

The picture of the New Inn (p. 88) is reprinted, by kind permission of the Cambridge University Press, from my *Story of Elizabethan Drama;* the illustration of the Hall of the Middle Temple (made before the Hall was badly damaged in a German air raid – it has since been restored) is reproduced by kind permission of the Masters of the Bench. The illustration of the Globe Playhouse is based on a model made by Dr J. C. Adams, who has very kindly allowed it to be used for this volume.

G.B.H.

CHAPTER I

The Legend of Shakespeare

No household in the English-speaking world is properly furnished unless it contains a copy of the Holy Bible and one of *The Works of William Shakespeare*. It is not always thought necessary that these books should be read in maturer years, but they must be present as symbols of Religion and English Culture.

Shakespeare has not always been so symbolic a figure. He was once an actor and a playwright, when neither actors nor the stage were regarded as respectable or of any importance. The notion that he was the supreme Genius of the English Race did not begin until he had been dead more than a century; but since then it has become so firmly accepted that no schoolboy can avoid a detailed study of at least one of his plays.

Nevertheless the first public notice of Shakespeare was hostile and unkind. In the autumn of 1592, Robert Greene, the most popular author of his generation, lay penniless and dying. Greene was a Cambridge man who had written several successful plays. The players had grown rich on the products of his brain, and now he was deserted and alone. He wrote a letter to three of his friends who had likewise helped to make the fortunes of the players, warning them to avoid his misfortunes. 'Is it not strange, that I, to whom they all have been beholding, is it not like that you to whom they all have been behold-

ing, shall (were ye in that case as I am now) be both at
once of them forsaken?' There was a greater grievance.
'Yes, trust them not,' Greene went on: 'for there is an
upstart Crow, beautified with our feathers, that with his
Tiger's heart wrapt in a Player's hide, supposes he is as well
able to bombast out a blank verse as the best of you: and
being an absolute *Johannes factotum*, is in his own conceit
the only Shake-scene in a country.'

At this time Shakespeare was only a beginner. The
Henry the Sixth plays, particularly the First Part (which
was first produced in March 1592) achieved considerable
success, but none of the plays which made him famous
had been written.

Six years later, in 1598, an earnest young student
named Francis Meres produced a book called *Palladis
Tamia;* an elaborate volume of what he called 'Simili-
tudes'. It was an anthology of specimens of fine writing
culled from more than a hundred and fifty authors. To
this he added a chapter called 'A Comparative Discourse
of our English poets with the Greek, Latin, and Italian
poets.' Shakespeare was easily his favourite amongst
English authors, praised as one of eight by whom 'the
English tongue is mightily enriched, and gorgeously invested in rare ornaments and resplendent habiliments.'
He was praised as one of six who had raised *monumentum
aere perennius;* as one of five who excelled in lyric
poetry; as one of thirteen 'our best for tragedy'; as
one of seventeen 'best for comedy'. Moreover Meres
picked him out for a special mention, not given to the
others:

As the soul of Euphorbus was thought to live in Pythagoras: so the sweet witty soul of Ovid lives in mellifluous and honey-tongued Shakespeare, witness his *Venus and Adonis*, his *Lucrece*, his sugared Sonnets among his private friends, &c.

As Plautus and Seneca are accounted the best for Comedy and Tragedy among the Latins: so Shakespeare among the English is the most excellent in both kinds for the stage. For Comedy, witness his *Gentlemen of Verona*, his *Errors*, his *Love's Labour's Lost*, his *Love's Labour's Won*, his *Midsummer Night's Dream*, and his *Merchant of Venice;* for Tragedy, his *Richard the II*, *Richard the III*, *Henry the IV*, *King John*, *Titus Andronicus*, and his *Romeo and Juliet*.

As Epius Stolo said that the Muses would speak with Plautus' tongue if they would speak Latin; so I say that the Muses would speak with Shakespeare's fine filed phrase if they would speak English.

Fourteen years later Shakespeare, now one of the older generation of dramatists, had lost something of his popularity. When John Webster published his play *The White Devil* (1612) he wrote a preface in which, by the way, he praised 'that full and heightened style of Master Chapman, the laboured and understanding works of Master Jonson, the no less worthy composures of the both worthily excellent Master Beaumont and Master Fletcher, and lastly (without wrong last to be named) the right happy and copious industry of M. Shakespeare, M. Decker, and M. Heywood.'

In 1623 (seven years after Shakespeare's death), appeared the First Folio, the first collection of his plays in one volume. It was prefaced by various tributes in verse, including a full-dress memorial Ode by Ben Jonson, magnificently superlative. In his private conversation Jonson was more critical. In the *Discoveries*, a collection of notes and jottings, posthumously published in 1641, he recorded:

> I remember, the Players have often mentioned it as an honour to Shakespeare, that in his writing, (whatsoever he penned) he never blotted out line. My answer hath been, would he had blotted a thousand. Which they thought a malevolent speech. I had not told posterity this, but for their ignorance, who choose that circumstance to commend their friend by, wherein he most faulted. And to justify mine own candour, (for I loved the man, and do honour his memory (on this side Idolatry) as much as any). He was (indeed) honest, and of an open, and free nature: had an excellent fancy; brave notions, and gentle expressions: wherein he flowed with that facility, that sometime it was necessary he should be stopped: *Sufflaminandus erat ;* as Augustus said of Haterius. His wit was in his own power; would the rule of it had been so too. Many times he fell into those things, could not escape laughter: as when he said in the person of Caesar, one speaking to him; *Caesar thou dost me wrong.* He replied: *Caesar did never wrong, but with just cause:* and such like; which were ridiculous. But he redeemed his vices, with his virtues. There was ever more in him to be praised, than to be pardoned.

In 1668 Dryden published his famous critical dialogue, the *Essay of dramatic poesy.* Shakespeare had now been dead fifty-two years, and during this time a second and a third edition of the Folio appeared. He was therefore about as near to Dryden's time as Tennyson is to ours. He was not yet a 'classic' whose perennial quality had been finally established, and no longer a modern. Dryden's estimate of him, expressed in the dialogue, was:

> To begin then with Shakespeare; he was the man who of all Modern, and perhaps Ancient Poets, had the largest and most comprehensive soul. All the Images of Nature were still present

to him, and he drew them not laboriously, but luckily: when he describes any thing, you more than see it, you feel it too. Those who accuse him to have wanted learning, give him the greater commendation: he was naturally learned; he needed not the spectacles of Books to read Nature; he looked inwards, and found her there. I cannot say he is every where alike; were he so, I should do him injury to compare him with the greatest of Mankind. He is many times flat, insipid; his Comic wit degenerating into clenches, his serious swelling into Bombast. But he is always great, when some great occasion is presented to him: no man can say he ever had a fit subject for his wit, and did not then raise himself as high above the rest of Poets,

Quantum lenta solent inter viburna cupressi.

The consideration of this made Mr Hales of Eton say, That there was no subject of which any Poet ever writ, but he would produce it much better done in Shakespeare; and however others are now generally preferred before him, yet the Age wherein he lived, which had contemporaries with him Fletcher and Jonson, never equalled them to him in their esteem: and in the last King's Court, when Ben's reputation was at highest, Sir John Suckling, and with him the greater part of the Courtiers, set our Shakespeare far above him.

Forty-one years later – in 1709 – Shakespeare was at length established as a classic when Nathaniel Rowe, a Restoration dramatist, brought out the first edited collection of his plays. Shakespeare now was sufficiently ancient for the public to need some information about him, and the taste of readers of plays had grown so much nicer that the earlier and simpler methods of printing were no longer suitable. Rowe added to his edition a short biographical introduction and some commendations of the passages which he most admired. He also considerably revised the text, adding place headings to the scenes and new stage directions. He was largely responsible for the form in which Shakespeare's plays are normally printed.

After Rowe, complete editions of the plays followed each other quickly, the most famous being those by Alexander Pope, 1723–5; Theobald, 1733; Hanmer, 1743–4; Dr Johnson, 1765; Edmund Malone, 1790. Between 1709 and 1799 no less than sixty editions of the plays, of all kinds including reprints, appeared.

During this century Shakespeare's reputation rapidly increased. Pope, though he was severe on Shakespeare's delinquencies – as he regarded them – praised lavishly.

If ever any Author deserved the name of an Original, it was Shakespeare. Homer himself drew not his art so immediately from the fountains of Nature, it proceeded through Egyptian strainers and channels, and came to him not without some tincture of the learning, or some cast of the models, of those before him. The Poetry of Shakespeare was Inspiration indeed: he is not so much an Imitator, as an Instrument, of Nature; and 'tis not so easy to say that he speaks from her, as that she speaks through him.

His Characters are so much Nature herself, that 'tis a sort of injury to call them by so distant a name as Copies of her. Those of other Poets have a constant resemblance, which shews that they received them from one another, and were but multipliers of the same image: each picture like a mock-rainbow is but the reflection of a reflection. But every single character in Shakespeare is as much an Individual, as those in Life itself; it is as impossible to find any two alike; and such as from their relation or affinity in any respect appear most to be Twins, will upon comparison be found remarkably distinct. To this life and variety of Character, we must add the wonderful Preservation of it; which is such throughout his plays, that had all the Speeches been printed without the very names of the Persons, I believe one might have applied them with certainty to every speaker.

The Power over our Passions was never possessed in a more eminent degree, or displayed in so different instances. Yet all along, there is seen no labour, no pains to raise them; no preparation to guide our guess to the effect, or be perceived to lead toward it: But the heart swells, and the tears burst out, just at the proper places: We are surprised, the moment we weep; and yet upon reflection find the passion so just, that we should be surprised if we had not wept, and wept at that very moment.

Dr Johnson wrote his famous preface to Shakespeare in 1765. Johnson never praised extravagantly, and he criticized freely. Shakespeare by this time was indisputably a classic, or as Johnson sonorously put it –

The Poet, of whose works I have undertaken the revision, may now begin to assume the dignity of an ancient, and claim the privilege of established fame and prescriptive veneration. He has long outlived his century, the term commonly fixed as the test of literary merit. Whatever advantages he might once derive from personal allusions, local customs, or temporary opinions, have for many years been lost; and every topic of merriment or motive of sorrow, which the modes of artificial life afforded him, now only obscure the scenes which they once illuminated. The effects of favour and competition are at an end; the tradition of his friendships and his enmities has perished; his works support no opinion with arguments, nor supply any faction with invectives; they can neither indulge vanity nor gratify malignity, but are read without any other reason than the desire of pleasure, and are therefore praised only as pleasure is obtained; yet, thus unassisted by interest or passion, they have passed through variations of taste and changes of manners, and, as they devolved from one generation to another, have received new honours at every transmission.

But because human judgement, though it be gradually gaining upon certainty, never becomes infallible; and approbation, though long continued, may yet be only the approbation of prejudice or fashion; it is proper to inquire, by what peculiarities of excellence Shakespeare has gained and kept the favour of his countrymen.

Nothing can please many, and please long, but just representations of general nature. Particular manners can be known to few, and therefore few only can judge how nearly they are copied. The irregular combinations of fanciful invention may delight awhile, by that novelty of which the common satiety of life sends us all in quest; but the pleasures of sudden wonder are soon exhausted, and the mind can only repose on the stability of truth.

Shakespeare is above all writers, at least above all modern writers, the poet of nature; the poet that holds up to his readers a faithful mirror of manners and of life. His characters are not modified by the customs of particular places, unpractised by the rest of the world; by the peculiarities of studies or professions, which can operate but upon small numbers; or by the accidents of transient fashions or temporary opinions: they are the genuine progeny of common humanity, such as the world will always supply, and observation will always find. His persons act and speak by the influence of those general passions and principles by which all minds are agitated, and the whole system of life is continued in motion. In the writings of other poets a character is too often an individual; in those of Shakespeare it is commonly a species.

By 1790 the learned critics, sage or pedantic, had said all that could then be said about Shakespeare. It was the turn of the antiquarians. Of these the most important were George Stevens and Edmund Malone. Stevens so early as 1766 realized that the text of Shakespeare had lost as well as gained by the reforming zeal of editors. He therefore reprinted twenty plays from the original Quartos. Malone, recognizing that the customs of the theatre had changed considerably in two centuries, wrote an historical account of the English stage which was not superseded for nearly a century.

With the turn of the century, and that revolution of interest not always very happily called the Romantic Revival, criticism of Shakespeare changed its tone. Shakespeare was no longer a great English dramatist, a faulty genius; he grew into a godlike figure. Samuel Taylor Coleridge was principally responsible for this conception.

Assuredly (he proclaimed in a lecture) that criticism of Shakespeare will alone be genial which is reverential. The Englishman, who without reverence, a proud and affectionate reverence, can utter the name of William Shakespeare, stands disqualified for the office of critic. He wants one at least of the very senses, the language of which he is to employ, and will discourse at best, but as a blind man, while the whole harmonious creation of light and shade with all its subtle interchange of deepening and dissolving colours rises in silence to the silent *fiat* of the uprising Apollo. However inferior in ability I may be to some who have followed me, I own I am proud that I was the first in time who publicly demonstrated to the full extent of the position, that the supposed irregularity and extravagances of Shakespeare were the mere dreams of a pedantry that arraigned the eagle because it had not the dimensions of the swan. In all the successive courses of lectures delivered by me, since my first attempt at the Royal Institution, it has been, and it still remains, my object, to prove that in all points from the most important to the most minute, the judgement of Shakespeare is commensurate with his genius – nay, that his genius reveals itself in his judgement, as in its most exalted form. And the more gladly do I recur to this subject from the clear conviction, that to judge aright, and with distinct consciousness of the grounds of our judgement, concerning the works of Shakespeare, implies the power and the means of judging rightly of all other works of intellect, those of abstract science alone excepted.

For a century after Coleridge it was still the fashion for those who spoke of Shakespeare in public to adopt the hushed tone and heightened phrases appropriate to a religious occasion.

Shakespeare to Coleridge was not so much a writer of plays as an emanation of the Godhead. Not much had been added to the knowledge of Shakespeare's biography since Rowe's day, and critics, romantically inclined, created their own image of a suitable Shakespeare. To Thomas Carlyle, in his quest for Heroes, Shakespeare was the Peasant Who Became A Prophet.

Whoever looks intelligently at this Shakespeare may recognize that he too was a *Prophet*, in his way; of an insight analogous to the Prophetic, though he took it up in another strain. Nature seemed to this man also divine; *un*speakable, deep as Tophet, high as Heaven: 'We are such stuff as Dreams are made of!' That scroll in Westminster Abbey, which few read with understanding, is of the depth of any seer. . . .

Well: this is our poor Warwickshire Peasant, who rose to be Manager of a Playhouse, so that he could live without begging; whom the Earl of Southampton cast some kind glances on; whom Sir Thomas Lucy, many thanks to him, was for sending to the Treadmill! We did not account him a god, like Odin, while he dwelt with us; – on which point there were much to be said. But I will say rather, or repeat: In spite of the sad state Hero-worship now lies in, consider what this Shakespeare has actually become among us. Which Englishman we ever made, in this land of ours, which million of Englishmen, would we not give up rather than the Stratford Peasant? There is no regiment of highest Dignitaries that we would sell him for. He is the grandest thing we have yet done. For our honour among foreign nations, as an ornament to our English Household, what item is there that we would not surrender rather than him? Consider now, if they asked us, Will you give up your Indian Empire or your Shakespeare, you English; never have had any Indian Empire, or never have had any Shakespeare? Really it were a grave question. Official persons would answer doubtless in official language; but we, for our part too, should not we be forced to answer: Indian Empire, or no Indian Empire; we cannot do without Shakespeare! Indian Empire will go, at any rate, some day; but this Shakespeare does not go, he lasts forever with us; we cannot give up our Shakespeare!

This was written in 1840. By 1875 the Great Figure had declined somewhat in stature. He was still romantic, but at least human. Scholars had been at work on Shakespeare's plays and the order of their writing had been fairly accurately established. In *Shakespeare, his mind and art*, Edmund Dowden made popular the notion that Shakespeare's plays show the development of his personality and reflect his private emotional life.

By the end of the century new materials for reconstructing Shakespeare's biography had accumulated, and were assembled in the *Life of William Shakespeare* by Sidney Lee, which for many years was regarded as the official biography. Lee had no romantic notions. He refused to believe that the personality of Shakespeare could be deduced from his works, and so, falling back on external facts of biography, he concluded that Shakespeare was a fine specimen of the Industrious Boy Who Got On:

A village youth, whose parents' material fortunes steadily declined in his early manhood, he injudiciously married as a mere boy, as boys sometimes will, a woman eight years his senior. Then he left his family in the country to make a career for himself in London. He was stagestruck and longed to act and write plays. In London, after a short interval, his triumphs as a dramatist gained for him an assured position in theatrical circles. He never obtained much reputation as an actor. Evidence of his professional progress makes it clear that he was singularly industrious, singularly level-headed, and amply endowed with that practical common sense which enables a man to acquire and retain a moderate competence. His financial rewards were substantial. He husbanded his pecuniary profits; he purchased houses and lands in his native place, whither he returned while yet middle-aged to enjoy a placid retirement.*

Lee's *Life of Shakespeare* first appeared in 1898. It was often reprinted and enlarged, and became a portly, impressive volume; but the critical reader on closer study found that many of his pronouncements were not statements of proved fact but guesses. After a while an acute scepticism developed when on page after page confident statements were qualified with 'there is little room for doubt that', 'it was doubtless', 'it is possible'. Hence there arose a reaction against all biographies of Shakespeare and a general feeling that, after all, nothing was really known about him.

Lee's *Life* was superseded in 1930 by Sir Edmund Chambers' two volumes, *William Shakespeare: a Study of Facts and Problems*. This was not so much a biography, as a monumental collection of every document, fact, and legend connected with Shakespeare, and with its four-volume predecessor, *The Elizabethan Stage*, gave students a set of invaluable reference books.

Elizabethan and other Essays, p. 86.

CHAPTER II

Materials for the Life of Shakespeare

To those who have not studied Elizabethan records it seems surprising and mysterious that there should be a dearth of intimate information about Shakespeare: so famous an Englishman, and such an unsatisfactory biography. Yet there is no mystery, for even in the lives of the greatest and most spectacular persons of the time there are many gaps. No one yet knows, nor ever will know, the private life of Queen Elizabeth I herself: and even such details as the date and place of the marriage of the Earl of Essex or of Sir Walter Raleigh are missing.

Nowadays it is easy to compile the biography of a modern dramatist. The essential facts of his life, his birth, his progress at school, at the university, and elsewhere, his marriage, and his death, are available in public records. While he is alive a number of the facts of his life will be given in *Who's Who*. His plays, as they come out, are noticed in newspapers and periodicals, and a little research in the files of old newspapers will show when the run of any particular play began and ended. Probably he will have given interviews, and when he dies journalists and critics hasten to write obituary notices and to record their impressions of his personality. He will certainly have written letters, which will be carefully preserved, for the letters of eminent authors are commercially valuable. Enough material will thus be provided for anyone to write quite a considerable Life.

Little of this material remains for the biographer of dramatists of the seventeenth century. The parish registers record the dates of baptism, marriage, and burial, but many of the registers are lost. There were no newspapers, very few diaries, and few individuals wrote chatty letters. Players and dramatists were regarded as persons of dubious standing, about whom no one was likely to be much interested unless they were concerned with some scandal or were made the victims of some scurrilous joke. Moreover, literary persons are seldom spectacular. The man who leads a life of heroic action has neither the time, nor usually the desire, to express himself in writing. Those who gallop down valleys of death do not usually sing about it. It is gentle poets living placidly in country rectories or suburban lodgings who write glorious and heroic ballads, as *The Charge of the Light Brigade*, or *Ye Mariners of England*. To be a great writer a man must spend much of his time at a table in the laborious act of writing, which is not an exciting or a spectacular occupation. Unless a writer of former days leaves a diary, or (like Keats) writes many letters which his friends will keep, or attracts a biographer (as Dr Johnson attracted Boswell), or meets a note-taker (as Ben Jonson met William Drummond of Hawthornden), or (like Christopher Marlowe) is in trouble with the authorities, the interesting details of his life vanish as soon as those who knew him die. Even to-day, when a literary man has news value, most of his readers will know little more of him than can be amply contained on a postcard. Of Shakespeare's life the records are far fuller than might be expected.

The main sources for a biography of Shakespeare are of four kinds.* First, and most important, are documentary records. These are definite and reliable, but usually dull, records of dates and facts. Thus, the parish register of Stratford-on-Avon gives the date (and therefore fact) of the baptism of William Shakespeare and of his brothers and sisters, the date of burial of himself, and of his father, mother, and other relatives. His name is to be found in some records of lawsuits either as plaintiff, witness, or defendant. In the accounts of the Court of Queen Elizabeth and King James the sums paid to his Company are noted. His will survives in Somerset House. There are many of these records.

The second kind of evidence is tradition. Traditions are of varying value, and frequently cannot be either tested or trusted. There is only one contemporary anecdote of Shakespeare recorded in the diary of John Manningham, a barrister; it is possibly an invented jest.

UPON a time when Burbage played *Richard III* there was a citizen grew so far in liking with him that before he went from the play she appointed him to come that night unto her by the name of Richard the Third. Shakespeare, overhearing their conclusion, went before, was entertained, and at his game ere Burbage came. Then a message being brought that Richard the Third was at the door, Shakespeare caused return to be made that William the Conqueror was before Richard the Third.

*All the relevant records are made fully available for students in *William Shakespeare: a study of facts and problems* by E. K. Chambers, which should be consulted for further details.

John Aubrey, a gentleman of the Restoration period, and a great collector of gossip, recorded a few anecdotes in his notebook, including traditions which he gathered at second and third hand from an old actor called William Beeston, who was the son of one of Shakespeare's fellow actors.

Betterton, a famous actor of Restoration times, went down to Stratford-on-Avon to examine the town records; and there he collected from local inhabitants some stories which he handed over to Nathaniel Rowe, who used them in his biographical introduction. Other anecdotes were current in the early part of the eighteenth century, and are recorded by Pope, Dr Johnson, and others.

The third source is literary. There are a number of references to Shakespeare in the writings of his contemporaries, and many more to his plays and characters. Most of them are literary and give no indication of what the man himself was like.

The fourth source of information is his work – the plays and the sonnets. The plays by themselves are not reliable material for a biographer. Shakespeare has said so much that it is impossible to know when he himself is speaking out of his own experience or creating experiences proper to his characters, but it is, and must be, generally true that no writer who portrays a great variety of characters and shows acquaintance with almost the whole range of human experience can have lived all his life in a narrow or confined environment. All great writers to some extent betray their origin. It is not difficult to guess that Jane Austen lived in a narrow circle or that the social background of Thackeray differed considerably from that of Dickens.

From the town records of Stratford-on-Avon it is clear that Shakespeare's family was of good middle-class stock. Shakespeare was neither a 'peasant', nor a 'village lad', nor 'the Stratford clown'. Stratford-on-Avon in the sixteenth century was a small but important country town, and John Shakespeare, his father, was one of the wealthiest citizens who held in turn the chief municipal offices of the place. He had married about 1557, Mary, the daughter of Robert Arden, who belonged to an ancient and distinguished Catholic family which suffered during the religious persecutions in Queen Elizabeth's reign. It is probable from recent researches that John Shakespeare himself was a Catholic, and that William was brought up in the Old Faith. John and Mary Shakespeare had at least eight children, William being the third child and eldest son. He was baptized in the Parish Church of Stratford-on-Avon on 26 April 1564.

There are no records of his boyhood; it would be surprising if there were. A good education was available at the grammar school, of which the head masters were competent scholars from Oxford and Cambridge. Nor were the better-class inhabitants of Stratford either bookless or illiterate. Several of Shakespeare's younger contemporaries and friends of the family went up to Oxford University.

In the ecclesiastical records of Worcester there is a bond dated 27 November 1582, indemnifying the Bishop of Worcester in any action that might arise by means of any pre-contract, consanguinity, affinity or by any other lawful means if William Shakespeare (his name is spelt Shagspere) and Ann Hathaway are married. The sureties were Fulke Sandall and John Richardson, friends of the bride. Shakespeare was aged 18½, and Ann, if the dates on her gravestone are correct, was aged 26. Nor was Ann Hathaway a peasant. Visitors to Stratford-on-Avon go to Shottery to see 'Ann Hathaway's Cottage', but the house is very far from being a cottage. It is the dwelling of a yeoman of means, as can be seen from the carved four-poster bed, and the panelling. There is no need to senti-mentalize the courtship, for the wedding seems to have been hasty. Five months later, on 26 May 1583, Susanna, their first child, was baptized, and on 22 February 1585, twins, Hamnet and Judith, were baptized. Apart from these records no fact in Shakespeare's early biography is recorded in any official document.

It is not known when Shakespeare first appeared in London. The essential years, when most men collect their experiences, are missing. There are various traditions: that he was obliged to leave Stratford because he was in trouble for poaching deer from Sir Thomas Lucy, the great man of those parts; that for a time he was a school-master in the country; that he first entered the theatre in some mean employment. But they do not account for everything.

It is not until 1592 that Shakespeare emerges as a per-son at the centre of English life. He was then aged 28. Nor is this ignorance confined to Shakespeare. Very little is known of what was happening in the Elizabethan theatres before 1592, although at this time there were three London theatres and several London companies, who must between them have been producing at least fifty new plays a year. Yet of the plays written for the professional companies between 1560 and 1590 less than half a dozen have survived in print. Hitherto no one thought that such plays were worth printing, reading, or recording. Critics assume that in the public theatres all plays were crude doggerel until Christopher Marlowe first showed his fellows how to write blank verse in *Tamburlaine*, and that Kyd's *Spanish Tragedy* and Greene's *Friar Bacon* were quite new kinds. It may be so, but there is no evidence. Accounts of what happened in the Elizabethan theatre before 1592 are, in fact, guesswork; but from this date onwards detailed records begin, and the development of British drama, though there are many gaps, can be traced.

From 1592 to 1602 Henslowe's *Diary* (see p. 47) gives a fairly complete picture of theatrical conditions and of the output of the companies with which he was connected. Unfortunately the Lord Chamberlain's Company, in which Shakespeare became a sharer, did not act in Henslowe's theatres, nor indeed did it come into existence until 1594.

From this time onwards there are many records of Shakespeare's name, and since it is sometimes questioned whether there are any reliable facts about him it is advisable to record some of the more important.

On 18 April 1593, Shakespeare's first poem, *Venus and Adonis*, was entered for publication in the Stationers'

Register, and soon afterwards printed, with a dedication to Henry Wriothesly,* Earl of Southampton:

Right Honourable,

I know not how I shall offend in dedicating my unpolished lines to your lordship, nor how the world will censure me for choosing so strong a prop to support so weak a burden: only, if your honour seem but pleased, I account myself highly praised, and vow to take advantage of all idle hours, till I have honoured you with some graver labour. But if the first heir of my invention prove deformed, I shall be sorry it had so noble a godfather, and never after ear so barren a land, for fear it yield me still so bad a harvest. I leave it to your honourable survey, and your honour to your heart's content; which I wish may always answer your own wish and the world's hopeful expectation.

Your honour's in all duty,
WILLIAM SHAKESPEARE

The poem was immediately popular, and during the next few years was reprinted nine times. It was much praised, and established Shakespeare's reputation as a poet.

There was very little playing throughout 1593, for a particularly bad outbreak of the plague occurred. The theatres were shut up and the players went on tour. On 9 May 1594, Shakespeare's second poem, *The Rape of Lucrece*, was published. This also was dedicated to the Earl of Southampton, but in far warmer terms:

The love I dedicate to your lordship is without end; whereof this pamphlet, without beginning, is but a superfluous moiety. The warrant I have of your honourable disposition, not the worth of my untutored lines, makes it assured of acceptance. What I have done is yours; what I have to do is yours; being part in all

*Pronounced 'Risley'.

I have, devoted yours. Were my worth greater, my duty would show greater; meantime, as it is, it is bound to your lordship, to whom I wish long life, still lengthened with happiness.

Your lordship's in all duty,

WILLIAM SHAKESPEARE

In the summer of 1594 the playing companies, which had been badly disorganized by the plague, began to drift back to London. For a few days Edward Alleyn, the great tragedian, ran a combined company made up of the Lord Chamberlain's and the Lord Admiral's players at a theatre in Newington Butts. During these few days Henslowe records that they played *Hamlet*, *The Taming of the Shrew*, and *Titus Andronicus*. The arrangement did not last long, and two new companies were formed. Alleyn went to play at the Rose Theatre and formed a new Lord Admiral's Company. Later in the autumn some of his former associates, including Richard Burbage and William Kemp, went to the Theatre in Shoreditch and there established a new Lord Chamberlain's Company. To this company Shakespeare now belonged, and henceforward his life is bound up with it and actual records accumulate.

During the Christmas holidays of 1594–5, the Company acted twice at Court. There is an entry in the Chamber Accounts:

To William Kempe, William Shakespeare, and Richard Burbage, servants to the Lord Chamberlain, upon the Council's warrant dated at Whitehall 15 March 1594[–5] for two several comedies or interludes showed by them before her Majesty in Christmas time last past, viz. upon St Stephen's day and Innocents' day, £13 6s. 8d., and by way of her Majesty's reward £6 13s. 4d.

The Company acted regularly at Court at Christmas time, but as the later payments were made to John Heming on their behalf Shakespeare's name is not mentioned in the accounts.

On 11 August 1596, the burial of Hamnet, son of William Shakespeare, is recorded in the Stratford Parish register.

On 20 October 1596, William Dethick, Garter Principal King of Arms, issued a grant of a coat of arms to John Shakespeare of Stratford-on-Avon

whose parents and late grandfather for his faithful and valiant service was advanced and rewarded by the most prudent prince, King Henry the Seventh, of famous memory, sithence which time they have continued at those parts being of good reputation and credit; and that the said John hath married the daughter and one of the heirs of Robert Arden of Wilmcote, in the said county, esquire; and for the encouragement of his posterity, to whom these achievements by the ancient custom of the Laws of Arms, may descend; I the said Garter King of Arms have assigned, granted, and by these presents confirmed; This shield or coat of arms, viz.: Gold, on a bend sables, a spear of the first, steeled argent. And for his crest or cognizance, a falcon, his wings displayed, argent, standing on a wreath of his colours; supporting a spear gold steeled as aforesaid, set upon a helmet with mantels and tassels as hath been accustomed and doth more plainly appeareth depicted on this margin. Signifying hereby and by the authority of my office aforesaid ratifying that it shall be lawful for the said John Shakespeare gentleman and for his children, issue and posterity (at all times and places convenient) to bear and make demonstration of the same blazon or achievement upon their shields, targets, escutcheons, coats of arms, pennons, guidons, seals, rings, edifices, buildings, utensils, liveries, tombs or monuments, or otherwise for all lawful warlike facts or civil use and exercises, according to the Laws of Arms and customs that to Gentlemen belongeth, without let or interruption of any other person or persons for use or bearing the same.*

William Shakespeare was thus entitled to call himself 'gentleman'. The coat of arms is emblazoned on his monument in Stratford-on-Avon Church.

On 4 May 1597, Shakespeare agreed to purchase from William Underhill, New Place, a large house in the centre of Stratford-on-Avon. The property included 'one messuage, two barns, and two gardens with the appurtenances', in return for which '*idem Willielmus Shakespeare dedit predicto Willielmo Underhill sexaginta libras sterlingorum*' – 'the same William Shakespeare gave the said William Underhill sixty pounds sterling.' The house has long since been demolished, but, as the foundations revealed, it was large, having a frontage of about sixty feet and a depth of about seventy.

On 29 August 1597, Andrew Wise entered for printing *The Tragedy of Richard the Second*. It was published soon after with the title page, 'The Tragedy of King Richard the Second. As it hath been publicly acted by the right Honourable the Lord Chamberlain his servants.' A second and third edition appeared in 1598 with the addition of 'By William Shakespeare'.

On 15 November 1597, the collectors of the subsidy for the ward of Bishopsgate, London, submitted a list of various persons from whom they could not collect their dues. Amongst those of St Helen's Parish was William

*Chambers, *op. cit.*, ii, 18.

Shakespeare, who owed 5s. Shakespeare's name appears in similar lists in 1598, 1599, and 1600.

In 1598 there was a considerable shortage of corn and a survey was taken of various holdings. In Stratford, William Shakespeare's name appears in the list taken on 4 February as holding ten quarters.

On 25 February 1598, Andrew Wise entered *The First Part of Henry the Fourth*, which appeared with the title 'The History of Henry the Fourth; With the battle at Shrewsbury, between the King and Lord Henry Percy, surnamed Henry Hotspur of the North. With the humorous conceits of Sir John Falstaff.'

On 22 July 1598, the Stationers' Register records that James Roberts entered 'for his copy under the hands of both the wardens, a book of the Merchant of Venice, or otherwise called the Jew of Venice, provided that it be not printed by the said James Roberts or any other whatsoever without licence first had from the Right honourable the Lord Chamberlain.' The book was afterwards transferred to Thomas Hayes, another printer, on 28 October 1600, who issued a Quarto with the title, 'The most excellent History of the Merchant of Venice. With the extreme cruelty of Shylock the Jew towards the said Merchant, in cutting a just pound of his flesh: and the obtaining of Portia by the choice of three chests. As it hath been divers times acted by the Lord Chamberlain his servants. Written by William Shakespeare.'

On 7 September 1598, Francis Meres' *Palladis Tamia*, with its praise of Shakespeare's work (see pp. 12–13), was entered for publication.

In September 1598, Ben Jonson's *Every Man in his Humour* was acted by the Lord Chamberlain's men. In the folio edition of Jonson's plays, published in 1616, it is noted:

This comedy was first acted, in the year 1598. By the then L. Chamberlain his servants. The principal comedians were:

Will. Shakespeare	Ric. Burbage.
Aug. Phillips.	Joh. Hemings.
Hen. Condell.	Tho. Pope.
Will. Sly.	Chr. Beeston.
Will. Kempe.	Joh. Duke.

On 25 October 1598, Richard Quiney, a Stratford friend, was in London, and wrote to Shakespeare the following letter:

Loving Countryman, I am bold of you as of a friend, craving your help with thirty pounds upon Mr Bushell's and my security or Mr Mytton's with me. Mr Rosswell is not come to London as yet, and I have especial cause. You shall friend me much in helping me out of all the debts I owe in London, I thank God, and much quiet my mind which would not be indebted. I am now towards the Court, in hope of answer for the despatch of my business. You shall neither lose credit nor money by me, the Lord willing, and now but persuade yourself so as I hope, and you shall not need to fear, but with all hearty thankfulness I will hold my time, and content your friend, and if we bargain farther you shall be the paymaster yourself. My time bids me hasten to an end, and so I commit this to your care and hope of your help. I fear I shall not be back this night from the Court. Haste. The Lord be with you and with us all, Amen. From the Bell in Carter Lane, the 25 October 1598. Yours in all kindness. Ryc. Quyney.

The letter was addressed 'To my loving good friend and countryman Mr Wm. Shakespeare deliver these.' It is now in the Birthplace Museum at Stratford.

Some time in 1598 Cuthbert Burby printed 'A Pleasant Conceited Comedy called, Love's Labour's Lost. As it was presented before her Highness this last Christmas. Newly corrected and augmented by W. Shakespeare.'

In 1599 a little octavo was printed with the title '*The Passionate Pilgrim* By W. Shakespeare.' It was a made-up volume, containing some sonnets from Shakespeare's plays, some sonnets which afterwards appeared in the volume of Sonnets, and a number of poems by other men.

On 23 August 1600, Andrew Wise and William Aspley entered in the Stationers' Register 'the second part of the history of King Henry the iiiith with the humours of Sir John Falstaff: written by Master Shakespeare.' It appeared with the title 'The Second Part of Henry the Fourth, continuing to his death, and coronation of Henry the Fifth. With the humours of Sir John Falstaff, and swaggering Pistol. As it hath been sundry times publicly acted by the right honourable, the Lord Chamberlain his servants. Written by William Shakespeare.'

On the same day Andrew Wise and William Aspley also entered *Much Ado about Nothing* 'written by Master Shakespeare.' Again the title page reads 'As it hath been sundry times publicly acted by the right honourable the Lord Chamberlain his servants. Written by William Shakespeare.'

On 8 October 1600, Thomas Fisher entered *A Midsummer Night's Dream*, which was published 'As it hath been sundry times publicly acted, by the right honourable, the Lord Chamberlain his servants. Written by William Shakespeare.'

On 8 September 1601, the burial of Mr John Shakespeare, Shakespeare's father, is recorded in the Stratford Parish register.

On 18 January 1602, *The Merry Wives of Windsor* was entered by John Busby. The text which he printed was pirated and hopelessly corrupt, but it gives some interesting facts. 'A most pleasant and excellent conceited comedy, of Sir John Falstaff, and the merry Wives of Windsor intermixed with sundry variable and pleasing humours of Sir Hugh the Welsh Knight, Justice Shallow, and his wise cousin M. Slender. With the swaggering vein of Ancient Pistol, and Corporal Nym. By William Shakespeare. As it hath been divers times acted by the right honourable my Lord Chamberlain's servants. Both before her Majesty, and elsewhere.'

On 1 May 1602, an agreement was made between William Combe of Warwick, Esquire, and John Combe of Old Stratford on the one part, and William Shakespeare of Stratford-on-Avon, Gentleman, of the other part, whereby the Combes 'in consideration of the sum of three hundred and twenty pound of current English money' sold to Shakespeare one hundred and seven acres of arable land in the parish of Old Stratford.

On 28 September 1602, Shakespeare acquired a cottage in Chapel Lane, Stratford-on-Avon. The transfer is recorded in the Court Roll of Rowington Manor: '*unum cotagium cum pertinenciis scituatum iacens et existens in Stratford super Avon, in quodam vico ibidem vocato Walkers Street alias Dead Lane, ad opus et usum Willielmi Shakespeare*'.

On 19 May 1603, letters patent were issued appointing

the former Lord Chamberlain's Company to be the King's Players. The patent records:

James by the grace of God, etc. To all Justices, Mayors, Sheriffs, Constables, Headboroughs, and other our officers and loving subjects, greeting. Know ye that We of our special grace, certain knowledge, and mere motion, have licensed and authorized and by these presents do license and authorize our servants Lawrence Fletcher, William Shakespeare, Richard Burbage, Augustine Phillips, John Hemings, Henry Condell, William Sly, Robert Armin, Richard Cowley and the rest of their associates, freely to use and exercise the art and faculty of playing Comedies, Tragedies, Histories, Interludes, Morals, Pastorals, stage plays, and such others, like as they have already studied or hereafter shall use or study, as well for the recreation of our loving subjects as for our solace and pleasure, when we shall think good to see them during our pleasure.

In 1603 Ben Jonson's *Sejanus* was acted. The folio edition of 1616 notes 'This Tragedy was first acted, in the year 1603. By the King's Majesty's servants. The principal tragedians were,

Ric. Burbage.	Will. Shakespeare.
Aug. Phillips.	Joh. Hemings.
Will. Sly.	Hen. Condell.
Joh. Lowin.	Alex. Cooke.'

Some time in 1603 a pirated, and very bad, text of *Hamlet* was printed entitled 'The Tragical History of Hamlet Prince of Denmark. By William Shakespeare. As it hath been divers times acted by his Highness' servants in the City of London: as also in the two Universities of Cambridge and Oxford, and elsewhere.' Another edition, the fullest of the early texts of *Hamlet* that exists, came out in 1604 with the title 'The tragical history of Hamlet, Prince of Denmark. By William Shakespeare. Newly imprinted and enlarged to almost as much again as it was, according to the true and perfect copy.'

In March 1604, King James made a 'royal proceeding' through the City of London. The players as servants of the Chamber were given red cloth for their liveries. The list of recipients each of four yards was: William Shakespeare, Augustine Phillips, Lawrence Fletcher, John Hemings, Richard Burbage, William Sly, Robert Armin, Henry Condell, Richard Cowley.

On 4 May 1605, Augustine Phillips was dying and made his will. He left bequests of gold pieces to his fellow actors. Shakespeare was mentioned first. 'I give and bequeath to my fellow, William Shakespeare, a thirty shilling piece in gold.' To Condell he also left a thirty-shilling piece; to five other members of the Company a twenty-shilling piece.

On 24 July 1605, Ralph Huband of Ippesley 'for and in consideration of the sum of four hundred and forty pounds of lawful English money' assigned to William Shakespeare one-half of all the tithes of Stratford, Old Stratford, Welcombe, and Bushopton, and half the tithes of the parish of Stratford-on Avon.

On 5 June 1607, the marriage of John Hall, Gentleman, and Susanna Shakespeare (Shakespeare's elder daughter) is recorded in the Stratford Parish register.

On 26 November 1607, was entered 'Master William Shakespeare his history of King Lear, as it was played before the King's Majesty at Whitehall upon Saint

Stephen's night at Christmas last, by His Majesty's servants playing usually at the Globe on the Bankside.' This information was repeated on the title page.

On 9 September 1608, the burial of Mary Shakespeare, widow (Shakespeare's mother), is recorded in the Stratford Parish register.

On 11 May 1612, Shakespeare was an important witness in a domestic lawsuit in which it was shown that about 1604 he was boarding in the house of Christopher Mountjoy, a Huguenot wig maker, near St Olave's Church, Cripplegate. Mountjoy's daughter married an apprentice named Stephen Bellott. Shakespeare had helped to make the match. In 1612 Bellott was suing his father-in-law for failing to give his daughter the portion agreed. Shakespeare was thus a principal witness. His evidence is headed 'William Shakespeare of Stratford upon Avon, in the County of Warwick, gentleman, of the age of forty-eight years or thereabouts, sworn and examined the day and year above said, deposeth and saith.' The answers to the five interrogatories were then recorded and he signed the document at the foot.

On 31 March 1613, the Steward of the Earl of Rutland paid to 'Mr Shakespeare in gold about My Lord's *impresa* 44s.; to Richard Burbage for painting and making it, in gold 44s.' The *impresa* was a shield painted with a device and mottoes borne at the tilting on the King's accession day.

On 28 January 1613, John Combe, a wealthy Stratford landowner, made his will, which included the bequest to 'Mr William Shakespeare five pounds'.

On 10 March 1613, Henry Walker, citizen and minstrel of London, assigned a dwelling place or tenement in the precinct of Blackfriars, 'part of which said tenement is erected over a great gate leading to a capital messuage', to William Shakespeare of Stratford-on-Avon, in the County of Warwick, Gentleman, William Johnson, citizen and vintner of London (and host of the Mermaid Tavern), John Jackson and John Heming of London, Gentlemen, for one hundred and forty pounds.

On 10 February 1616, the marriage of Thomas Quyny and Judith Shakespeare (Shakespeare's younger daughter) is recorded in the Stratford Parish register.

On 25 March 1616, Shakespeare executed his will. It is a lengthy document (now in Somerset House) on three sheets of parchment, each of which he signed. As it gives a clear picture of his family relationship, it is worth reprinting in full:

In the name of God, Amen! I William Shakespeare, of Stratford upon Avon in the county of Warr., gent., in perfect health and memory, God be praised, do make and ordain this my last will and testament in manner and form following. That is to say, First, I commend my soul into the hands of God my Creator, hoping and assuredly believing, through the only merits of Jesus Christ my Saviour, to be made partaker of life everlasting, and my body to the earth whereof it is made.

Item, I give and bequeath unto my daughter Judith one hundred and fifty pounds of lawful English money, to be paid unto her in the manner and form following; that is to say, one hundred pounds in discharge of her marriage portion within one year after my decease, with consideration after the rate of two shillings in the pound for so long time as the same shall be unpaid unto her after my decease, and the fifty pounds residue thereof upon her surrendering of or giving of such sufficient security as the overseers of this my will shall like of, to surrender or grant, all her estate and right that shall descend or come unto her after my decease, or that she now hath, of, in, or to, one copy-hold tenement, with the appurtenances, lying and being in Stratford upon Avon aforesaid in the said county of Warr., being parcel or holden of the manor of Rowington, unto my daughter Susanna Hall and her heirs forever.

Item, I give and bequeath unto my said daughter Judith one hundred and fifty pounds more, if she or any issue of her body be living at the end of three years next ensuing the day of the date of this my will, during which time my executors to pay her consideration from my decease according to the rate aforesaid. And if she die within the said term without issue of her body, then my will is, and I do give and bequeath one hundred pounds thereof to my niece Elizabeth Hall, and the fifty pounds to be set forth by my executors during the life of my sister Joan Hart, and the use and profit thereof coming shall be paid to my said sister Joan, and after her decease the said £50 shall remain amongst the children of my said sister, equally to be divided amongst them. But if my said daughter Judith be living at the end of the said three years, or any issue of her body, then my will is, and so I devise and bequeath the said hundred and fifty pounds to be set out by my executors and overseers for the best benefit of her and her issue, and the stock not to be paid unto her so long as she shall be married and covert baron; but my will is, that she shall have the consideration yearly paid unto her during her life, and, after her decease, the said stock and consideration to be paid to her children, if she have any, and if not to her executors or assigns, she living the said term after my decease. Provided that if such husband as she shall at the end of the said three years be married unto, or attain after, do sufficiently assure unto her and the issue of her body lands answerable to the portion of this my will given unto her, and to be adjudged so by my executors and overseers, then my will is, that the said £150 shall be paid to such husband as shall make assurance, to his own use.

Item, I give and bequeath unto my said sister Joan £20 and all my wearing apparel, to be paid and delivered within one year after my decease; And I do will and devise unto her the house with the appurtenances in Stratford wherein she dwelleth, for her natural life, under the yearly rent of 12d.

Item, I give and bequeath unto her three sons, William Hart, —— Hart, and Michael Hart, five pounds apiece, to be paid within one year after my decease.

Item, I give and bequeath unto the said Elizabeth Hall all my plate (except my broad silver and gilt bowl) that I now have at the date of this my will.

Item, I give and bequeath unto the poor of Stratford aforesaid ten pounds; to Mr Thomas Combe my sword; to Thomas Russell, esquire, five pounds; and to Francis Collins, of the borough of Warr., in the county of Warr., gent., thirteen pounds, six shillings, and eight pence, to be paid within one year after my decease.

Item, I give and bequeath to Hamlet Sadler xxvis. viiid. to buy him a ring; to William Reynolds, gent., xxvis. viiid. to buy him a ring; to my godson William Walker xxs. in gold; to Anthony Nash, gent., xxvis. viiid.; and to Mr John Nash xxvis. viiid.; and to my fellows John Heminge, Richard Burbage, and Henry Condell, xxvis. viiid. apiece to buy them rings.

Item, I give, will, bequeath, and devise unto my daughter Susanna Hall, for better enabling of her to perform this my will, and towards the performance thereof, all that capital messuage or tenement with the appurtenances, in Stratford aforesaid, called the New Place wherein I now dwell, and two messuages or tenements with the appurtenances, situate, lying and being in Henley Street, within the borough of Stratford aforesaid; and all my barns, stables, orchards, gardens, lands, tenements, and hereditaments whatsoever, situate, lying and being or to be had, received, perceived, or taken, within the towns, hamlets, villages, fields, and grounds of Stratford upon Avon, Old Stratford, Bushopton, and Welcombe, or in any of them in the said county of Warr. And also all that messuage or tenement, with the appurtenances, wherein one John Robinson dwelleth, situate, lying, and being in the Blackfriars in London, near the Wardrobe; and all my other lands, tenements and hereditaments whatsoever, to have and to hold all and singular the said premises, with their appurtenances, unto the said Susanna Hall, for and during the term of her natural life, and after her decease, to the first son of her body lawfully issuing, and to the heirs males of the body of the first son lawfully issuing; and for default of such issue, to the second son of her body lawfully issuing, and to the heirs males of the body of the second son lawfully issuing; and for default of such heirs, to the third son of the body of the said Susanna lawfully issuing, and of the heirs males of the body of the said third son lawfully issuing; and for default of such issue, the same so to be and remain to the fourth, fifth, sixth, and seventh sons of her body issuing one after another and the heirs males of the bodies of the said fourth, fifth, sixth and seventh sons lawfully issuing, in such manner as it is before limited to be and remain to the first, second and third sons of her body, and to their heirs males; and for default of such issue, the said premises to be and remain to my said niece Hall, and the heirs males of her body lawfully issuing; and for default of such issue, to my daughter Judith, and the heirs males of her body lawfully issuing; and for default of such issue, to the right heirs of me the said William Shakespeare for ever.

Item, I give unto my wife my second best bed with the furniture. Item, I give and bequeath to my said daughter Judith my broad silver gilt bowl. All the rest of my goods chattels, leases, plate, jewels, and household stuff whatsoever, after my debts and legacies paid, and my funeral expenses discharged, I give, devise and bequeath to my son-in-law, John Hall, gent., and my daughter Susanna his wife, whom I ordain and make executors of this my last will and testament.

And I do entreat and appoint the said Thomas Russell, esquire, and Francis Collins, gent., to be overseers hereof, and do revoke all former wills, and publish this to be my last will and testament. In witness thereof I have hereunto put my hand, the day and year first above written.

By me William Shakespeare.

On 25 April 1616, the burial of Will. Shakespeare, Gentleman, is recorded in the Stratford Parish Register.

These are but a selection of actual and indisputable records of various kinds which mention Shakespeare by name. They show that William Shakespeare of Stratford-on-Avon, after a youth and early manhood spent no one knows where, became a successful dramatist sometime before the autumn of 1592; that in the autumn of 1594 he was a member of the Lord Chamberlain's Company which became the King's Company in 1603; that he wrote plays for the Company which were popular; that he prospered and made money which he invested in property at Stratford; and that he died in his native town. From these beginnings it is not impossible to build up a fairly complete biography, for the life of the dramatist is bound up with the Company to which he belonged and for which he wrote his plays.

CHAPTER III

The Modern Approach to Shakespeare

I

SOME preliminary preparation is necessary to understand any great works of art, and especially those which belong to a past age. Shakespeare was regarded as a great writer from the first, and the history of Shakespearian criticism mirrors the changes in taste of the last 350 years. Since the beginning of the twentieth century there have been several new developments and changes of interest.

In the year 1904 there was published a series of lectures originally delivered in the University of Oxford which caused considerable stir at the time; the volume was entitled *Shakespearean Tragedy*, and it was written by Dr A. C. Bradley. The book was the culmination and the best example of over a century of Shakespearian criticism, which began with Maurice Morgann's *Essay on the dramatic character of Sir John Falstaff* (1777), and continued with Lamb and Coleridge, and throughout the nineteenth century. Dr Bradley's attitude, in general, was that the characters in Shakespeare's plays were real men and women whose emotions, personalities, motives, and even past history, could be minutely examined, dissected, and discussed. Dr Bradley wrote before the present enthusiasm for psychology, but his lectures were in the main psychological. In their own way they were magnificent, and the general feeling at the time amongst critics and readers was almost one of despair that the last word had been said, on the greater tragedies at least, and that nothing more remained to be done.

Nevertheless, in the same year 1904, there appeared the first two volumes of two works which have actually revolutionized modern notions about Shakespeare and his plays. They were the edition of the works of the Elizabethan pamphleteer, Thomas Nashe, edited by R. B. McKerrow, and the *Diary* and *Papers of Phillip Henslowe*, edited by Dr W. W. Greg. Both were fine pieces of scholarship. McKerrow examined the different texts minutely, and by exact comparison and deduction he was able to reveal much that went on in the Elizabethan printing-houses, while by his illuminating commentary he illustrated contemporary thought and history. This work was one of the first great examples of the modern study of bibliography which showed scholars what could be recovered by exact examination of texts and manuscripts.

The *Diary* and *Papers* of Phillip Henslowe were important in another way. Henslowe was the owner of several London theatres: the Rose, the Fortune, and others. For a period of ten years, between 1592 and 1602, he kept an exact account in a large ledger of his dealings with the various companies that played at his theatres. This account book, known as *Henslowe's Diary*, is the most important document of Elizabethan stage history. In 1592 Edward Alleyn, the first Elizabethan tragic actor to become famous, married Henslowe's stepdaughter, and for the next twenty-four years Henslowe and Alleyn worked in close partnership. After Henslowe's death in 1616 the papers passed to Alleyn. Alleyn by this time was a wealthy man, and in his old age he founded the College of God's Gift at Dulwich. When he died he bequeathed his collection of pictures to his foundation, and by surprising luck his papers have survived. As well as the *Diary* they include contracts with actors, letters from dramatists, the agreement with the builder for building the Fortune Theatre, private letters, inventories of costumes and properties, and other documents which are invaluable.

Henslowe's *Diary* had been edited by 1845 by John Payne Collier, a fine Elizabethan scholar. Unfortunately Collier, for some reason, finding that his discoveries did not keep pace with his enthusiasms, began to invent Elizabethan documents and to forge additions in genuine manuscripts. When his forgeries were at last revealed his work was naturally discredited and his edition of the *Diary* was so suspected that little attention was paid to it. Dr Greg was easily able to clear the *Diary* of Collier's additions, and to show the importance of these documents for an understanding of the conditions of the Elizabethan stage. His edition of the *Diary* and *Papers* came out between 1904 and 1907. As a result scholars for a number of years had the field to themselves. It was quickly realized that once the conditions under which Shakespeare wrote were known, much light would be thrown on the making of his plays. For a time the philosopher – for Bradley was philosopher rather than scholar – gave way to the antiquarian.

To-day students of Shakespeare are interested mainly in three kinds of study which radiate from the plays. An intensive study of any one kind or of all may bring us nearer understanding – or farther away – as they are used and followed. These kinds of study may be labelled Scholarly, Literary, and Dramatic.

The scholar says in effect, 'This Shakespeare has been dead for more than three hundred years. Times, manners, and ideas have changed greatly. To understand him therefore we must know his environment and examine his plays in the conditions of their original composition.'

The attitude of the critic, on the other hand, is that great literature is timeless and therefore perpetually modern. He is not concerned with an antiquity but with certain works of dramatic art and how they concern him.

The producer and the actor, again, say, 'Our business is with the theatre of to-day, its customs and conventions, its staging and its audience. We must therefore act Shakespeare's plays in a manner which will be understood by a modern audience of mixed interests, knowledge, and appreciation – that is, if we produce them at all.'

2

Modern scholars, in studying Shakespeare's environment, are concerned with a wide variety of interests, which may be subdivided into three main branches of study.

(*a*) The first branch is the study of the conditions of dramatic production: the details of the construction, arrangement, and conventions of the Elizabethan stage; the organization and history of the dramatic companies; the actors themselves, their styles, and personalities; the audience and theatre-going public, its tastes and prejudices. These and other kindred matters will affect the writing and acting of a play. All are relevant even to an elementary understanding of Shakespeare's plays; for had he written for a modern stage the form and manner of his plays would have been quite different.

(*b*) Shakespeare's plays survive as printed texts. The conditions of publication are therefore important. The scholar must study the history of a play's script, and how Elizabethan plays were in fact written. He must examine the earliest texts to see whether there are traces of revision or collaboration. He must know something of the method of a printing-house, the habits of the reading public, the methods of the censor and how he worked. He must study the history of the text of a play itself from the time when the author first wrote it until, having passed through stage performance, it appeared as a printed Quarto; what happened between the printing of the Quarto of a separate play and the time when it was printed in the first collected edition of Shakespeare's works, the Folio of 1623; the changes that have occurred between the first printing of the Folio and the modern text. All these factors will affect the printed text which the reader of to-day uses, and which also gives the actor his lines for a performance on the stage.

(*c*) There are other factors relevant, but not so immediate. All dramatists are concerned with interesting

their audiences, and all drama directly or indirectly re-
flects the taste and ideas of its own time. The events great
and small that were happening around Shakespeare are
therefore directly or indirectly part of his material. The
scholar must know something of current notions and
topics, of wars, excitements, depressions, revolutions; of
passing feelings and literary fashions, for fashions in literature changed even more quickly in Shakespeare's time
than to-day. He must be familiar with the current ideas of
the times, of literary criticism, science, psychology,
history, morals, religion. All these affected Shakespeare
immediately; they passed through the filter of his personality and were largely the material of his drama; for
he, no less than other dramatists, supplied his audience
with thoughts which were immediately interesting and
exciting.

All these considerations are important for an intelligent
study of Shakespeare, and until we have some knowledge
of them we cannot fully understand and so appreciate his
plays.

It is obvious, for instance, at a first reading, that many
of Shakespeare's words have an essentially different meaning from modern usage. When Bottom says:

> And Phibbus' car
> Shall shine from far,

he is not referring to headlights. Similarly when Shakespeare used the word 'presently' it meant 'at once' and
not 'by-and-by'; in recent years the word has in America
come to mean 'at this time'. 'The humorous man' was not

the funny man of the party, but the melancholic, the eccentric. Such words are so entirely different in their meaning that they cause little difficulty, for in most editions there are notes and glossaries which will explain them.

Far more difficult, and often quite beyond recall, are the subtler differences, the associations and ideas that cluster round the commonest of words, such as 'king' or 'prince', 'father', 'daughter', 'wife'. Whatever nowadays may be the normal associations of the word 'king', they are hardly those expressed (probably by Shakespeare himself) in the play of Sir Thomas More:

> For to the King God hath His office lent
> Of dread, of justice, power and command,
> Hath bid him rule, and will'd you to obey;
> And, to add ampler majesty to this,
> He hath not only lent the King His figure,
> His throne and sword, but given him His own Name,
> Calls him a god on earth. What do you then
> Rising 'gainst him that God Himself installs,
> But rise 'gainst God?

In this conception of the monarchy there is little room for a salaried official called the Leader of Her Majesty's Opposition.

Nor again, even in old-fashioned families, does a modern father arrange a marriage for his daughter without consulting her, as Old Capulet does for Juliet, or Touchstone for his daughter in the play of *Eastward Ho* (1605). Nor, having arranged it, would he usually expect to receive this answer: 'Sir, I am all yours: your body gave me life: your care and love, happiness and life: let your virtues still direct it, for to your wisdom I wholly dispose myself.' In Shakespeare's time such notions were commonly associated with the words 'king', 'daughter', and 'father'.

In another direction modern scholarship has been profoundly altered by a renewed interest in the study of early texts. The most stimulating pioneer work here was by A. W. Pollard. In *Shakespeare's Fight with the Pirates* (1917) he showed that the earliest of Shakespeare's texts were often set up directly from Shakespeare's own manuscript by a printer who followed his copy closely. This, at the time, was a revolutionary idea, for when Dr Bradley produced his lectures it was generally felt that the Shakespearian text had been established and was unalterable. Generations of editors from the early eighteenth century onwards had edited Shakespeare's texts, emending difficult passages and formalizing them, so that the Globe or Cambridge text was regarded as the 'authorized version' of Shakespeare. Now the new and exact study of bibliography, exemplified in McKerrow's edition of Nashe, showed that there was a wealth of interest in the detailed comparison and examination of early texts. The result was that when scholars again began to look at the early Quarto and Folio texts with respectful interest, and not merely to despise them as the semi-illiterate efforts of bungling printers, all kinds of new discoveries were made.

It is indeed a revelation to read a familiar play for the first time in a Quarto or Folio text. The reader finds himself at once in the atmosphere of the Globe Theatre. Most plays in the original texts have no scene divisions; many even have no act divisions. There are none of those place headings which editors have added – Act 1, Scene i, *A Room in the Palace*: Act iv, Scene iii, *Another Part of the Field*. These did not exist in the original text because in the Elizabethan theatre there was no scenery and little physical indication of a change of locality. The reader realizes at once how editors have tampered with the texts, sometimes by brilliant guessing producing sense from corrupt passages, but more commonly by erecting an eighteenth-century façade to an Elizabethan play.

Antony and Cleopatra is an extreme example of editorial method. The play is commonly criticized because there are too many scenes. Thus in the Fourth Act there are, according to the Globe text, no less than thirteen scenes:

i. *Before Alexandria. Caesar's Camp.*
ii. *Alexandria. A Room in the Palace.*
iii. *The Same. Before the Palace.*
iv. *The Same. A Room in the Palace.*
v. *Alexandria. Antony's Camp.*
vi. *Before Alexandria. Caesar's Camp.*
vii. *Field of Battle between the Camps.*
viii. *Under the Walls of Alexandria.*
ix. *Caesar's Camp.*
x. *Between the two Camps.*
xi. *Alexandria. A Room in the Palace.*
xii. *The Same. Another Room.*
xiii. *The Same. A Monument.*

In the Folio text there are no scene divisions at all.

The editorial principle was that when all characters have gone off the stage a scene ends. A scene must take place somewhere. Therefore the place must be indicated.

But in Shakespeare's plays, as originally intended for the stage, scenes were not place-scenes but rather person-scenes, and here at the crisis of the fortunes of Antony, Caesar, and Cleopatra, Shakespeare shows how each rises or declines at the supreme moment. In the Folio text there are therefore no scene divisions, no place headings. The scenes, in fact, are concerned with Caesar: Antony and Cleopatra: the common soldiers: Antony and Cleopatra: Antony: Caesar: the battle: Antony and Cleopatra: Enobarbus: the defeat of Antony: Cleopatra hearing the news: Antony's attempt to stab himself: Cleopatra's distress: Antony's death. It is a dramatic technique which can be understood only when we remember that the play is Elizabethan and written for an Elizabethan stage. If Act IV is split into thirteen different localities, then the attention of the reader or spectator is distracted from the persons to the places, and the play becomes unreadable and unactable.

Another offence of editors of the eighteenth and nineteenth centuries was that they tampered with the punctuation and the arrangement of the lines. Often they were justified, but their enthusiasm was excessive. Mr Percy Simpson, in a little book called *Shakespearean Punctuation* (1911) first pointed out that the punctuation in the First Folio was dramatic and not grammatical. In the Folio especially, and the Quartos more casually, the texts were punctuated for recitation. The punctuation is not always consistent or sound, and it is very doubtful if Shakespeare was responsible for it; but certainly the punctuation is contemporary and inserted by those who knew and did their business well. Later editors, by normalizing Shake-spearian punctuation to modern grammatical usage, have wiped out many of the original subtleties. In the best Folio texts we are not only in imagination in the Globe Theatre but can also hear the speeches spoken as Shake-speare's actors delivered them.

Some examples will make this clear. The opening lines of *Twelfth Night* in the accepted text are punctuated thus:

> If music be the food of love, play on;
> Give me excess of it, that, surfeiting,
> The appetite may sicken, and so die.
> That strain again! It had a dying fall:
> O! it came o'er mine ear like the sweet sound
> That breathes upon a bank of violets,
> Stealing and giving odour.

In the Folio these lines are punctuated:

> If music be the food of Love, play on,
> Give me excess of it: that surfeiting,
> The appetite may sicken, and so die.
> That strain again, it had a dying fall:
> O, it came o'er my ear, like the sweet sound
> That breathes upon a bank of violets;
> Stealing, and giving odour.

Antony's speech over Caesar's corpse is punctuated in the accepted text:

> Friends, Romans, countrymen, lend me your ears;
> I come to bury Caesar, not to praise him.
> The evil that men do lives after them,
> The good is oft interred with their bones;
> So let it be with Caesar. The noble Brutus
> Hath told you Caesar was ambitious;

If it were so, it was a grievous fault,
And grievously hath Caesar answer'd it.
Here, under leave of Brutus and the rest, —
For Brutus is an honourable man;
So are they all, all honourable men, —
Come I to speak in Caesar's funeral.
He was my friend, faithful and just to me:
But Brutus says he was ambitious;
And Brutus is an honourable man.
He hath brought many captives home to Rome,
Whose ransoms did the general coffers fill:
Did this in Caesar seem ambitious?
When that the poor have cried, Caesar hath wept;
Ambition should be made of sterner stuff:
Yet Brutus says he was ambitious;
And Brutus is an honourable man.
You all did see that on the Lupercal
I thrice presented him a kingly crown,
Which he did thrice refuse: was this ambition?
Yet Brutus says he was ambitious;
And, sure, he is an honourable man.
I speak not to disprove what Brutus spoke,
But here I am to speak what I do know.
You all did love him once, not without cause:
What cause withholds you then to mourn for him?
O judgement! thou art fled to brutish beasts,
And men have lost their reason. Bear with me;
My heart is in the coffin there with Caesar,
And I must pause till it come back to me.

In the Folio text the punctuation of the speech runs
thus:

Friends, Romans, countrymen, lend me your ears:
I come to bury Caesar, not to praise him:
The evil that men do, lives after them,

The good is oft interred with their bones,
So let it be with Caesar. The noble Brutus,
Hath told you Caesar was ambitious:
If it were so, it was a grievous fault,
And grievously hath Caesar answer'd it.
Here, under leave of Brutus, and the rest
(For Brutus is an honourable man,
So are they all; all honourable men)
Come I to speak in Caesar's funeral.
He was my friend, faithful, and just to me;
But Brutus says, he was ambitious,
And Brutus is an honourable man.
He hath brought many captives home to Rome,
Whose ransoms, did the general coffers fill:
Did this in Caesar seem ambitious?
When that the poor have cried, Caesar hath wept:
Ambition should be made of sterner stuff,
Yet Brutus says, he was ambitious:
And Brutus is an honourable man.
You all did see, that on the Lupercal,
I thrice presented him a kingly Crown,
Which he did thrice refuse. Was this ambition?
Yet Brutus says, he was ambitious:
And sure he is an honourable man.
I speak not to disprove what Brutus spoke,
But here I am, to speak what I do know;
You all did love him once, not without cause,
What cause withholds you then, to mourn for him?
O Judgement! thou art fled to brutish beasts,
And men have lost their reason. Bear with me,
My heart is in the coffin there with Caesar,
And I must pause, till it come back to me.

The differences here are slight but subtle. It is just the difference between a piece of music as played by an amateur and by a master.

The attitude of the scholar is, then, that Shakespeare was an Elizabethan with the advantages and limitations of his age. His plays were subject to the conditions of his times. He was, in short, a man who provided the plays for a particular company of actors. It is a sound kind of study revealing much and vastly increasing the enjoyment of a play. Scholarship can be misused, and if the scholar merely regards Shakespeare as an antiquity and forgets that he was not much more than a man who wrote plays for an Elizabethan theatre, it is the business of the critic and producer to correct that impression.

3

The second kind of study is critical. By critical is implied a study of Shakespeare which is not concerned mainly with Shakespeare in his own times or with the Elizabethan stage, but with the plays as specimens of dramatic poetry.

Of critical approaches there are mainly two. The first is 'appreciation', that is, 'literary criticism' as it has hitherto been generally known – the judging or appraising of a work of art by certain recognized principles and standards of taste. There has been a continuous stream of criticism of this kind. The modern method of criticism of Shakespeare started with Maurice Morgann's criticism of Falstaff, and has continued ever since. Since Bradley, Sir Walter Raleigh's *Shakespeare* in the 'English Men of Letters' series is perhaps the most popular of the general studies. Another lively and human book, Q's *Shakespeare's Workmanship*, rather lowered the tone of exaltation to be found in Bradley, and reminded us once more that Shakespeare was after all a man of the theatre. Of modern critics Mr T. S. Eliot and Mr Middleton Murry have their particular following. 'Appreciation' is the commonest kind of criticism, and every year critics add a number of contributions to the pile.

The latest development of critical interest, however, is in a close and very detailed study of Shakespeare's actual poetic technique. It varies from the elaborate card-indexing of Shakespeare's poetic imagery adopted by Caroline Spurgeon in *Shakespeare's Imagery* (1934) to the personal and subjective essays of Mr Wilson Knight in *The Wheel of Fire*, *The Imperial Theme*, and other volumes, a process which he calls 'interpretation'. This kind of critical approach has for the last twenty-five years been very popular with the younger critics.

This kind of study is primarily concerned with style. Great poets are individuals both in personality and in expression. Poetic style consists — apart from the content — largely of individual rhythms, and more particularly of an individual use of images (which used to be called 'metaphors' and 'similes'). A poet's metaphors will spring from his personality and experience. A bookish poet, such as Milton or Pope, will draw most of his images from the books that he has read: he and his readers will take an acute pleasure in these literary echoes. Less learned and more original poets will use images which spring from their own personal experiences, or, to quote Caroline Spurgeon, the poet 'may be, and in Shakespeare's case is, almost entirely objective in his dramatic characters and their views and opinions, yet, like the man who under

60

stress of emotion will show no sign of it in eye or face, but will reveal it in some muscular tension, the poet unwittingly lays bare his own innermost likes and dislikes, observations and interests, associations of thought, attitudes of mind and beliefs, in and through the images, the verbal pictures he draws to illuminate something quite different in the speech and thought of his characters.'

This is an exciting prospect. Whenever we read Shakespeare we shall always be coming across some little betrayal, sublime or homely, particularly when an image is repeated in a different form and seems to express some peculiar like or dislike of a poet; it will be revealing something that presses on his mind. Thus Henry V, discoursing on the responsibilities of a king, says:

> Not all these, laid in bed majestical,
> Can sleep so soundly, as the wretched slave:
> Who with a body fill'd, and vacant mind,
> Gets him to rest, cramm'd with distressful bread.

A similar thought comes into Hamlet's mind at a tragic moment. He is about – so he thinks – to slay his uncle, and he remembers the death of his own father:

> He took my father grossly, full of bread.

Obviously a full meal of bread had an unpleasant significance for Shakespeare. It throws an unexpected sidelight on his digestion and Mrs Shakespeare's baking; but this is perhaps a frivolous way of looking at the problem!

Miss Spurgeon's method was to card-index, analyse, and tabulate all Shakespeare's images, and, as part of the process, to analyse the imagery used by other Elizabethan dramatists. The result was to confirm certain impressions : that Shakespeare has far more images drawn from sport than other dramatists, that Marlowe's imagery is predominantly drawn from the classics, and so forth. It is a fascinating pastime, and one of the few forms of literary research that can be carried out at home. One requires only a volume of Shakespeare's plays and a number of cards for the card-index.

The values and limitations of this kind of study lie in its being mechanical; an absolutely mechanical scientific collection of statistics of this kind reveals many of the processes of the human mind which would escape notice altogether in ordinary reading. It cannot be carried too far, for a poetic image is not a simple or mechanical expression, but, especially in Shakespeare's later period, a fusion of all kinds of sparkling ideas. It is often quite impossible to separate the particular images in a clot of imagery such as :

> Come thick Night,
> And pall thee in the dunnest smoke of Hell,
> That my keen knife see not the wound it makes,
> Nor Heaven peep through the blanket of the dark,
> To cry, hold, hold.

In this passage neither *knife* nor *blanket* can suitably be classified under 'Images drawn from domestic articles'.

Nevertheless, within reason, a study of imagery will give results similar to chemical analysis. The water of a well, when analysed, will show so much of this, so much of that, and perhaps a minute trace of zinc. The analysis is entirely objective; it is not the business of the chemist to say how zinc should be present in the water. The history of the well will show that, some six months before, a bucket had accidentally been dropped in it. A study of Shakespeare's imagery will show many of his experiences, but not how and when he came by them.

Occasionally, when the material exists, it is possible to trace the actual source of a poetic image. Professor J. Livingstone Lowes studied Coleridge's *Kubla Khan* and *The Ancient Mariner*. He had as external evidence Coleridge's notebooks, which showed what Coleridge had been reading at the time. Moreover, from Dorothy Wordsworth's *Journals* and similar sources Coleridge's external experiences were recorded. As a result, in *The Road to Xanadu*, Professor Lowes was able to trace back almost every idea and phrase in *Kubla Khan* and *The Ancient Mariner* to its original source, and thereby to present a fascinating picture of how the poet's mind worked. Similarly, by comparing Keats' letters and his poetry, Mr Middleton Murry was able to show how Keats' mind worked.

Unfortunately there are no notebooks for Shakespeare, and any deductions must be largely guesswork. One cannot even tell whether an image is negative or positive. A man may be full of images of sport either because he is himself a great sportsman, or because he is feeble-bodied and envies those of better physique. Sporting journalists are not necessarily expert sportsmen. Nor are those who make a particular study of Shakespeare's imagery agreed amongst themselves.

Once, having a private theory of my own, based on the fact that Shakespeare's images drawn from the sea and war indicated that at some time or other he had seen war and the sea at first hand, I put it to two authorities on Shakespearian imagery. I asked each of them the same question: 'Do you, from your intensive study of Shakespeare's imagery, gather that he had personal experience of the sea?' The one replied, 'Of course'; and the other, 'Certainly not.'

From this one can deduce that, just as a poetic image comes from a poet's experience, which includes the books that he has read, so also the perception of an image and of its significance by readers or hearers comes from their experience. Unless the critic has known the same kind of experiences as the author he will miss many images and their significance. As Keats put it in a letter, when writing of Wordsworth, 'We find what he says true as far as we have experienced, and we can judge no further but by larger experience – for axioms in philosophy are not axioms until they are proved upon our pulses. We read fine things, but never feel them to the full until we have gone the same steps as the author. – I know this is not plain; you will know exactly my meaning when I say that now I shall relish Hamlet more than I have ever done.'

Here again, scholarship is important, for until the reader himself has some knowledge of Elizabethan idiom – and this requires a considerable knowledge of the Elizabethan background – he cannot appreciate the full meaning of many Elizabethan images. Macbeth, for instance,

WILLIAM SHAKESPEARE
(*From the engraving in the First Folio*)

returning from the murder of Duncan with his hands covered with blood, and dazed with horror at what he has seen and done, murmurs:

> One cried God bless us, and Amen the other,
> As they had seen me with these hangman's hands.

To a modern reader there is no reason why a hangman should not have clean hands; it would show a lack of delicacy for him to exercise his profession unwashed. But to Shakespeare's audience the phrase had a ghastly significance, for in executions for treason it was the hangman's business to tear out the victim's entrails before hacking the body into quarters.

Again, such a phrase as 'on your allegiance' or 'on your peril' means very little to a modern reader. If used in official documents which retain ancient formulas, the words mean little more than 'otherwise you will be liable to a penalty not exceeding £5.' To an Elizabethan 'on your allegiance' was the solemnest form of command; to disobey it was to commit high treason and to risk the ghastly penalty.

4

The third approach is the dramatic. Just as critical and scholarly notions about Shakespeare have changed in the last fifty years, so also has the fashion of producing his plays in the modern theatre. Henry Irving died in 1905. He was the great leader of one school of Shakespearian presentation, magnificent, gorgeous, and elaborate. The productions of Herbert Beerbohm Tree in the decade before the First World War were even more spectacular, and are still talked of by veteran theatre-goers. It is a sign of complete change of taste that such expensive realism is nowadays regarded as ridiculous. Real rabbits are not necessary to create the atmosphere for *A Midsummer Night's Dream*, nor are fountains of real water with live goldfish necessary for *Antony and Cleopatra*. It is easy to mock this kind of production, and there are certain grave objections to it because the plays have to be cut, altered, and re-arranged to allow the big scenes to be set. Moreover if our eyes are fully occupied with all the gorgeous details of costume or procession, our ears are distracted from the words. Nevertheless the principles behind the method were not necessarily so unsound at the time. Shakespeare's plays, it was assumed, were in themselves no longer act-able but they were classics. They contained beauties and passages which everyone knew, and they could be illus-trated. The attitude of Tree and of Irving towards their public was much the same as that of a Hollywood pro-ducer; 'Give them the best bits – something gorgeous to look at – and you have done well by them.'

The revolution against these methods came with the Shakespearian productions of Harley Granville-Barker in 1910–13, especially of *Twelfth Night*. They were the most important productions for a hundred years, not only because they were beautiful in themselves, but because for the first time since the seventeenth century Shake-speare's plays were played just as they were written, and not cut and re-arranged to suit the scene-shifter. Without unduly horrifying his audiences, Granville-Barker evolved settings which allowed him to give the whole play entire and quickly. For *Twelfth Night* the main setting was a formal conventional garden with Noah's ark trees and a central staircase branching out right and left, which needed little re-arrangement. For the smaller scenes – the drinking scene for instance – he inserted a little tapestried room and not the usual baronial hall, which made the whole affair cosy and hearty. He suppressed all the traditional foolery, the candles-to-bed business of Toby and Andrew, and he produced the play as a whole, as a symphony. The result, astonishing at the time, was that *Twelfth Night*, instead of being just a romp, became exquisitely beautiful and hauntingly sad.

In these productions Granville-Barker demonstrated what had hitherto hardly been realized, that Shakespeare did indeed know how to write plays. Everyone granted that he was a great poet who had provided a marvellous quiverful of quotations for public speakers, that he was a philosopher, and of course that he had quite a deep knowledge of human nature, but very few (and certainly not such critics as A. C. Bradley) realized the possibilities of his plays being superb stage dramas if only they could be produced as he wrote them to be played.

The Granville-Barker *Twelfth Night* was a compromise between modern and Elizabethan. It combined the simplicity and rapid action of the Elizabethan with the lavishness of the modern; for it was magnificently costumed and lovely to the eyes. Since that time most producers have followed the main principle demonstrated by Granville-Barker. Whatever the setting, the play is acted as a whole, in its original pattern and with its full plot. The good producer begins by assuming that Shakespeare knew his business as a writer of good plays, and not merely of fine speeches, and therefore that the production must be a competent rendering of the score.

CHAPTER IV

Shakespeare's Company

THE company of players known first as the Lord Chamberlain's Players, and later as the King's Men, came into existence in the summer of 1594. There had been severe outbreaks of the plague in 1592 and 1593, and at such times the London playhouses were closed. The companies were badly disorganized by these continual interruptions. When at last playing could be resumed in London, there was a considerable regrouping. Edward Alleyn, now at the peak of his fame as an actor of tragedy parts, formed a new company under the patronage of the Lord Admiral, which opened at the Rose Theatre on the Bankside south of London Bridge. A few weeks later a new Lord Chamberlain's Company began to play at the Theatre at Shoreditch, north of the city. This playhouse was owned by James Burbage.

The Theatre had been built in 1576. In the 1570s there had been much friction between the playing companies and the Lord Mayor and Aldermen of the City of London. Hitherto, players had acted to the public in various City inns. It was not a desirable arrangement, and the City authorities did their utmost to prevent it. The objections to plays were those perpetual to any form of public entertainment which attracts rowdy crowds. Not only were there riots and disturbances from time to time, but the players sometimes indulged in unseemly comment on their betters, and, above all, there was a perpetual risk of the plague, which was easily spread in crowded assemblies. The Lord Mayor succeeded in preventing the players from acting within the jurisdiction of the City. The legal boundaries of the City, however, were small, and London was already spreading out well beyond its limits. To the north in the Middlesex suburbs, and south of the river in the Surrey suburbs, the jurisdiction lay with the Magistrates of Middlesex and Surrey, who were far more complacent.

In 1576 James Burbage acquired a twenty-one year's lease of a piece of land in Shoreditch, north of the city, and there erected the first permanent playhouse, which was named the Theatre. The venture was a success. Other playhouses followed. By 1594 there were also the Curtain in the Shoreditch neighbourhood, and the Rose on the Bankside, the suburb which had grown up at the south end of London Bridge.

James Burbage had originally been chief player of the great Earl of Leicester. His son, Richard Burbage, was now making a name for himself as a tragic actor. He had learnt his business under Alleyn, but they parted company; and now, in the autumn of 1594, Richard Burbage became the leader of a new Lord Chamberlain's Company. This Company also included Will Kemp, and Shakespeare. William Kemp in his own way was as famous as Alleyn. He was the clown of the Company. He had already played considerably on the Continent. His style of acting, to which there are a number of references, was broad: he was a low comedian, and he preferred to have the stage to himself so that he might amuse the people by his own crude and at times gross antics. Kemp was particularly famous for jigs. At this time it was still the fashion to end the afternoon's entertainment with a jig, which was a short song and dance with one or two characters miming some simple (and usually bawdy) tale.

Between 1592 and 1593 both Marlowe and Greene, hitherto the only English writers to make much name for themselves on the public stages, had died. Kyd, the author of the famous *Spanish Tragedy*, died before the end of 1594. Thus, for a few months, the Chamberlain's Men had a great advantage in Shakespeare, who was the only dramatist with any considerable reputation.

By 1594 Shakespeare had already written three parts of *Henry VI*, and *Richard III*, which told the story of the beginnings of the Wars of the Roses, and their final end, when Henry Tudor defeated Richard III at the Battle of Bosworth Field, *Titus Andronicus*, *The Two Gentlemen of Verona*, *Love's Labour's Lost*, *The Taming of the Shrew*, and *The Comedy of Errors*.

The Lord Chamberlain's Company acted *The Comedy of Errors* at Christmas, 1594, as part of the elaborate revels of Gray's Inn at Court. One of their earliest successes was *Romeo and Juliet*, which perfectly accorded with the mood of the moment for sonneteering and love poetry. Soon afterwards Shakespeare wrote *A Midsummer Night's Dream*. apparently for some special performance at a wedding, and about 1595 he continued the story of the troubles of the fifteenth century, by showing how they all began when

Richard II was unlawfully deposed, and afterwards mur-
dered by his cousin, Henry Bolingbroke, thereby bringing
down the curse upon the House of Lancaster which was
the theme of the plays of the Wars of the Roses. *King John*
and *The Merchant of Venice* were written probably in 1596.

Shakespeare had certainly prospered in these months.
The application for the coat of arms made in his father's
name in 1596 shows that the family considered itself sufficiently well-to-do to claim the right to be officially recognized as gentlefolk. The coat was granted by the Heralds,
and the motto chosen was significant – 'Non sanz droict';
what history lies behind this self-conscious challenge is
not known, though much can be guessed.

There was trouble for Shakespeare in this year, 1596,
though the details are regrettably brief. In 1931 Professor
Leslie Hotson published his discovery of a new reference
to Shakespeare. It is a record that William Wayt claimed
sureties of the peace against William Shakespeare, Francis
Langley, Dorothy Soer, and Ann Lee, for fear of death,
and so forth. Unfortunately nothing is definitely known of
the cause of William Wayt's anxiety.

The Company also had its disappointments in 1596.
James Burbage, who in his own way had a touch of genius,
realized that conditions in the playgoing world were
changing. In 1580 men of taste and education had little
good to say of the theatres. Sir Philip Sidney, in his
Apology for Poetry, had condemned them heartily for their
lack of propriety. Now, however, that good writers had
been attracted to write plays, young men of fashion and
intelligence were becoming interested in the theatres.

Burbage saw that they, rather than the general public, were the most paying patrons of the theatre. But gentlemen of taste were put off by the mixed and noisy crowds who paid their pennies to stand in the yard of the public playhouse. Some few years before, a very successful private theatre had existed for a few years in the Blackfriars. It had been managed by John Lyly and the actors were choir boys from St Paul's and the Chapel Royal. Lyly's venture had come to an end about 1590. While it lasted it catered solely for a better-class audience.

The lease of the ground on which the Theatre stood was coming to an end, and James Burbage thought to revive the idea of the private theatre. Plays in the public theatres were acted in the open air. A private indoor theatre would not be affected by the weather, and it was better to attract a small audience paying good prices than a larger audience paying their pennies. He therefore acquired the refectory of the old Blackfriars Monastery – the site is now occupied by The Times building – and proceeded at considerable expense to turn it into an indoor playhouse.

Blackfriars at this time was a fashionable residential quarter. The aristocratic inhabitants complained that the playhouse would be a great nuisance with its noises of drums and trumpets, and its crowds of people. Accordingly the Privy Council gave orders that Burbage was not to use the building for playing, and the venture was for a long time a complete loss.

The year 1597 also was full of anxiety for the Lord Chamberlain's Men. The lease of the ground upon which the Theatre stood had originally been taken out for twenty-one years. It expired in April 1597. By the conditions of the lease, either Burbage could renew the lease on agreed terms, or he must remove the playhouse building before its expiry. If he did not fulfil these conditions then the building was appropriated to the ground landlord, a man called Giles Alleyn. Alleyn proved difficult. He knew that the players did not wish to rebuild their theatre, but he refused to offer terms which were in any way acceptable. The wrangle continued for many months.

Meanwhile, on 28 July 1597, all theatres were peremptorily shut by order of the Privy Council. The trouble arose through the Earl of Pembroke's players, who were playing at the Swan (a new playhouse erected on the Bankside) and put on a play called *The Isle of Dogs*. It was a very seditious and topical comedy, and its authors were Thomas Nashe and Ben Jonson. Jonson at this time was an actor in Pembroke's Company. The Privy Council were so angry that they ordered playing to cease forthwith, and Jonson and two fellow-actors, Gabriel Spencer and Robert Shaa, were put in prison. There was no further playing until the autumn.

Meanwhile, Shakespeare had gained new notoriety. For some reason, which does not seem quite obvious nowadays, the subjects of Queen Elizabeth in the 1590s found certain close parallels between the political situation in the reign of Richard II and in their own times. It was never safe to make direct comment on current affairs, but historical plays and books which seemed to offer oblique political criticism were usually popular. Somehow it was felt that Queen Elizabeth resembled Richard II, and many of the followers of the Earl of Essex, who was now beginning to fall out of favour, saw in him a second Bolingbroke.

In August 1597 Andrew Wise printed Shakespeare's *Richard II*. It was a most popular publication, and in six months went into three editions. The play, however, was not complete, for the deposition scene was left out.

About this time, Shakespeare began to write the sequel to *Richard II* in the first part of *Henry IV*. It was another stage in the story of the curse on the House of Lancaster. Naturally, any story about Henry introduced his madcap son Prince Hal, who was a popular and legendary hero. He had already appeared on the stage in an old play called *The Famous Victories of Henry V*, where his companion in mischief was called Sir John Oldcastle. When Shakespeare wrote the play in the autumn of 1597, London was swarming with captains who had returned with Essex from the expedition known as the Islands Voyage. One of these Shakespeare began to envisage as Prince Hal's companion. He called him Sir John Oldcastle. This caused trouble. The real Sir John Oldcastle was burnt for his Lollard principles during the reign of Henry V, and therefore secured his place in *Foxe's Book of Martyrs*. Oldcastle was known also as Lord Cobham, and the Lord Cobham of Shakespeare's day, an unpleasant young man who had just succeeded to the title, objected. Shakespeare was obliged, therefore, to alter the name of Oldcastle, who henceforward became Falstaff.

In this play, too, he parodied one of his own most effective scenes. In the passage where the Prodigal Prince rehearses his interview with his father, Shakespeare made Falstaff play the stage King 'in Cambyses' vein'. It was an obvious and broad parody of the style and acting of Edward Alleyn. The parody was successful. Shakespeare followed the first part of *Henry IV* with a Second Part, into which he introduced a new character, Ancient Pistol, who stalked about the stage, strutting and behaving in Alleyn's manner with a vocabulary which was largely composed of ranting misquotations from plays in the repertory of the Admiral's Men.

The year 1598 was exciting in many ways for the Lord Chamberlain's Company. Falstaff from the very first was a great success. Then in the early autumn the Company put on a play by a new author who was beginning to make his name. Ben Jonson, after his imprisonment over the *Isle of Dogs* affair, had joined the Lord Admiral's Men and was writing plays for them; but for some reason he quarrelled with the Admiral's Men, with the result that his first good play, *Every Man in His Humour*, was offered to the Chamberlain's Men. They acted it in September with considerable success. The play had a sensational advertisement. Gabriel Spencer, who had been Jonson's companion in misfortune over the *Isle of Dogs*, waited for Jonson as he was coming from the playhouse and quarrelled with him. The two men fought each other in Hoxton Fields, and Spencer was killed. Jonson was again put in prison, but he was able to plead benefit of clergy and after a short time was released.

Matters with Giles Alleyn were now coming to a head. The lease of the Theatre ground had long expired and nothing was settled. For the last few months the Company had left the Theatre and were playing in the Curtain. It was now clear that Alleyn meant to take advantage of the clause in the original lease, and unless something drastic was done the Burbages would lose their valuable property.

The chief sharers in the Company, Richard Burbage and his brother Cuthbert, Shakespeare, John Hemings, Augustine Phillips, Thomas Pope, and Will Kemp, agreed to finance a new playhouse. In this new arrangement the Burbages held two and a half shares and the others one apiece. In addition, as playing members of the Company, each held an actor's share of the takings. A new site was found on the Bankside not far from the Rose Theatre, and the lease was signed on 25 December 1598.

Three days later the two Burbages and a number of their friends, all armed, together with Peter Street, a builder who was to build the new playhouse, appeared outside the Theatre and proceeded to tear it down. As the Theatre was a timber building this did not take long. Giles Alleyn himself was away from London, but his people dared not interfere. The timber was then carried across the Thames and dumped on the new site. Meanwhile, until the new house was ready, the Company were still playing at the Curtain, where, early in April 1599, *Henry V* was produced.

The new playhouse – now the finest in London – was ready about July: it was called the Globe. By this time the Chamberlain's Men had a fine repertory, and their latest plays included the two parts of *Henry IV* and *Henry V* and Jonson's *Every Man in his Humour*. To these were soon added Jonson's *Every Man out of his Humour*, Shakespeare's *As You Like It*, and *Julius Caesar*.

The competition with the Admiral's Men now became acute. Even while the Chamberlain's Men were separated by the river and the City, there had been some feeling, but now that the two companies were playing side by side the Admiral's Men soon felt the effects. Accordingly, in October, they set their dramatists to work to provide a counter-attraction. This was a new and more or less true version of the story of Sir John Oldcastle.

The play was put on for the first time on 1 November, and Henslowe, to show his appreciation, awarded the players ten shillings as a gift. It was, however, soon obvious that the competition of the Chamberlain's Men would be too much for the Admiral's, and Alleyn decided to build a new theatre north of the river in the parish of St Giles. There were many vexatious delays, but ultimately, late in 1600, the new playhouse called the Fortune was finished and opened.

In the autumn of 1599 both Admiral's and Chamberlain's Men began to suffer from a new rival. William Stanley, Earl of Derby, was an enthusiastic amateur of plays. In November, at considerable cost, he revived the company of the Children of Paul's. The children of the choir of St Paul's Cathedral had not attempted to produce plays for the last nine years, but now the Earl of Derby set them going again, and John Marston, a young barrister who had recently distinguished himself as a virulent satirist, was brought in to provide them with plays. The investment was a success. As James Burbage had foreseen three years before, there was a great opening for small private playhouses which would cater solely for gentlemen.

Others were interested by the new playhouse. Henry Evans, who had been Lyly's partner in the former Boys' Company, saw a chance of starting another company of Boys. He went into partnership with the Master of the Chapel Royal, Nathaniel Giles. Giles, by authority of his office, was empowered to impress likely boys into the Royal choir. Evans had his eye on the empty Blackfriars Theatre, which was a considerable burden to the Burbages, for they had to find the rent but could make no use of it. The objections to the presence of professional players in the Blackfriars neighbourhood did not apply so strongly to semi-private performances by choir boys. Evans therefore hired the Blackfriars Playhouse from the Burbages on 2 September 1600, and in a very short time he had established another Children's Company, which was immediately prosperous.

Soon Ben Jonson, who seldom stayed long with one company, joined the Children of Blackfriars to provide plays for them. Marston offended Jonson by producing in his play *Histriomastix* a character called Chrysoganus, which was an obvious, though flattering, imitation of Jonson's Macilente in *Every Man out of his Humour*. Jonson took umbrage. He attacked Marston in his next play by making unpleasant hits at his person and his style. Marston countered, and for the next year a regular war of the Theatres was waged between the two Boy Companies.

Early in 1601 the Chamberlain's Men were again in trouble. The fortunes of the Earl of Essex were now at their lowest; and he and his followers were planning a revolution. As part of their propaganda some of Essex's friends approached the Company and asked them to act *Richard II*. The players were not enthusiastic. The play had not been acted for some time and they did not believe that it would prove a good draw, but when Essex's friends promised to augment the takings with 40s. they agreed. Accordingly *Richard II* was acted on 7 February 1601. The next day was Essex's futile rising. When the Privy Council began to make enquiries the players were closely questioned about this affair, which was regarded as very sinister, but no action was taken and their indiscretion was overlooked.

Meanwhile the bickerings of the Children of Paul's and the Blackfriars were exciting genteel audiences. Both the professional Companies – Admiral's and Chamberlain's – felt the loss of their best customers. At last Ben Jonson, who was tiring of the struggle, decided to produce a play which would finally extinguish Marston. It was called *Poetaster*, and came out in the autumn of 1601. It was put on by the Children of Blackfriars.

The Chamberlain's Men and the Paul's Boys united to retaliate. They hired Thomas Dekker, who had hitherto written for the Admiral's, to compose an answer to Ben Jonson. His play was called *Satiromastix* and followed *Poetaster* very shorty. Dekker was so much more skilful at abuse that Ben Jonson retired from play-writing for a couple of years. Shakespeare himself seems to have taken some part in this controversy. In the Christmas holidays the undergraduates of St John's College, Cambridge, acted a College play called *The Return from Parnassus*. They impersonated Burbage and Kemp who were brought in to give a lesson in acting, and they made Kemp say, 'That Ben Jonson's a pestilent fellow; he brought up Horace giving the poet a pill, but our fellow Shakespeare has given him a purge that made him bewray his credit.' This play or scene has apparently disappeared.

During these months Shakespeare wrote *Hamlet*, which was full of references to the events of the time.* About the same time he also wrote *Twelfth Night*, which was performed in the Hall of the Middle Temple on 2 February 1602.

In March 1603 Queen Elizabeth fell ill. As there was considerable doubt about the succession in the minds of the people at large, there was great alarm. On 19 March the Privy Council, who of late years had become increasingly suspicious of the theatres, ordered all playing to cease. Five days later, Queen Elizabeth died.

The death of the Queen actually advanced the fortunes of the players, and especially of the Chamberlain's Men. One of the first acts of the new King was to take the Company under his own protection. On 19 May they became the King's Men, and a licence (see p. 38) was granted to them. There was, however, little playing that summer, for once again the plague broke out in the City of London and continued for nearly a year. The players, as usual, were obliged to go on tour, but at Christmas time they

*For details see *Hamlet* in the Penguin Shakespeare.

received a summons to come down to Wilton near Salisbury and there to play before the King and his Court. For this they received £30, for their expenses and for acting one play. By Christmas the plague was abating and the Court was held at Hampton Court. The Company acted six times in the Christmas holidays before the Court.

About this time Shakespeare wrote *Measure for Measure*, a sombre comedy in a new vein. In the autumn and winter of 1605–5 the players were much in request. On the 1st November they played *Othello* in the Banqueting House at Whitehall; on the 4th, *The Merry Wives of Windsor*; on the 26th December the *Comedy of Errors*; early in January *Love's Labour's Lost* and *Henry V*. On the 10th February they played *The Merchant of Venice*, which so pleased King James that he ordered it to be played again on the 12th.

Shakespeare was now apparently writing less for the Company, but in 1606 and again in 1607 he wrote at least two plays. *Lear* and *Macbeth* were probably written in 1606, and *Antony and Cleopatra* and *Coriolanus* probably in 1607.

There were many changes and developments during these years. The Boys' Companies flourished for some years and attracted to themselves some of the best writers of the time. Chapman was writing regularly for them, and in 1607 began the famous partnership of Francis Beaumont and John Fletcher, who wrote *Philaster* and *The Maid's Tragedy* for the Blackfriars Children.

In 1608, however, the Children of Blackfriars were abruptly turned out of their playhouse. From the first they had been a nuisance to the authorities. The temptation to appeal to their small audiences by constantly commenting on current affairs was too great. In 1605 they had produced *Eastward Ho!*, a play written by Jonson, Marston, and Chapman, in which they even had the impudence to mimic King James's Scots accent; it caused considerable trouble. In 1608 they offended unforgivably. Chapman wrote a play called *The Conspiracy and Tragedy of Charles, Duke of Byron*, which dealt with the rebellion and death of the Duke in Paris. It was recent history, and concerned living persons. Chapman even brought on the stage the reigning French King, Henry IV, together with his Queen and his mistress. In one scene the Queen was shown boxing the ears of her rival. The French Ambassador protested, and the Boys were forbidden to act the play. Soon afterwards, when the Court had left London, they disobeyed this order. As a result the Company was for a time dissolved. Evans and his partners in the Blackfriars were now left with an empty playhouse on their hands, and they asked the Burbages to release them from their agreement.

The King's Men welcomed the chance. Conditions had changed considerably in the last eleven years, and there was no longer any serious opposition to the players occupying the Blackfriars playhouse. Moreover, the Globe Theatre was found to have its drawbacks. It was built on marshy ground, which in winter became very muddy. Accordingly, in August 1608, Richard Burbage took into partnership his brother Cuthbert, Shakespeare, Hemings, Condell, and Sly, and his former tenant Evans. They took over the private playhouse for winter use, and, in addition, they purchased the plays belonging to the Children and agreed to employ their dramatists.

The different conditions in the private playhouses are reflected in the plays produced after the death of Queen Elizabeth. The Globe Theatre was open to the air and plays were acted by daylight. In the Blackfriars Theatre plays were acted by candlelight. Far more elaborate stage effects were therefore possible. Moreover, as the players now mainly concerned themselves with a better-class audience, drama tended to become more sophisticated and less public.

Shakespeare appears to have written little between 1608 and 1610. Then in 1610 and 1611 he wrote his three last plays, *Cymbeline*, *The Winter's Tale*, and *The Tempest*. *The Tempest* was acted for the King on 1 November 1611, and *The Winter's Tale* on 5 November. Shakespeare, however, seems now to have spent most of his time at Stratford. On 2 July 1613, his career as a dramatist was symbolically ended by the destruction of the Globe Theatre. The Players were acting *Henry VIII* with considerable magnificence. The disaster caused much comment, and there are a number of references to it. The most detailed is in a letter written by Sir Henry Wotton:

Now, to let matters of State sleep, I will entertain you at the present with what hath happened this week at the Bankside. The King's Players had a new play, called *All is True*, representing some principal pieces of the reign of *Henry VIII*, which was set forth with many extraordinary circumstances of pomp and majesty, even to the matting of the stage, the Knights of the Order, with their Georges and Garter, the guards with their embroidered coats, and the like: sufficient in truth within a while to make greatness very familiar, if not ridiculous. Now, King *Henry* making a masque at the Cardinal Wolsey's house, and certain cannons being shot off at his entry, some of the paper, or other stuff, wherewith one of them was stopped, did light on the thatch, where being thought at first but an idle smoke, and their eyes more attentive to the show, it kindled inwardly, and ran round like a train, consuming within less than an hour the whole house to the very ground.

This was the fatal period of that virtuous Fabrique; wherein yet nothing did perish, but wood and straw, and a few forsaken cloaks; only one man had his breeches set on fire, that would perhaps have broiled him, if he had not by the benefit of a provident wit put it out with Bottle-Ale.

It is possible that the disaster was greater than Wotton realized, for it may be that a number of Shakespeare's plays perished in the fire.

CHAPTER V

The Elizabethan Playhouse

DRAMA, of all forms of art, is most immediately affected by material circumstance. The poet or the novelist can wait for recognition, perhaps for years, but a dramatist, and especially one who is also a sharer in the playhouse and company which produces his plays, cannot afford a failure. He must please his public or he will go bankrupt. He appeals, not to future ages, but to the audience of the afternoon. His plays therefore must be written to suit the stage on which they will be performed, the company which is to act them, and the audience which will pay to see them.

Until James Burbage built the Theatre in 1576 Elizabethan players had no permanent home. They were accustomed to act on a variety of stages. They gave private performances in the great halls of noblemen's houses or one of the Queen's palaces, or the Inns of Court, and they acted in public in Town Halls and inn yards, or in any place where they could erect a stage and collect a crowd.

Little is known for certain of the design of Burbage's Theatre, or indeed of the exact details of the other playhouses, but the general features can be deduced from the many stage directions in the original Quartos, or the First Folio of Shakespeare's plays, to go no farther. The existence, for instance, of two doors and an upper stage is shown by such directions as *Enter one Citizen at one door*, *and another at the other*, and *Enter Richard aloft, between two Bishops.**

Only one contemporary sketch of the stage exists. It is of the Swan, and was made from memory by a Dutch traveller named De Witt in 1596; but his memory seems to have been as slight as his drawing.

THE SWAN THEATRE: A SKETCH MADE IN 1596

James Burbage's Theatre apparently combined the features of the inn yard and the great hall. Inns in the sixteenth century were built round a courtyard, and the

*Richard III, II. iii and III. vii.

guests' rooms opened on to galleries which looked down into this yard. The stage was erected at one end, on barrel heads or trestles, and spectators from the street stood in the yard, whilst the more respectable spectators sat in the galleries. The best surviving specimen of a medieval inn,

THE COURTYARD OF THE NEW INN AT GLOUCESTER

where also plays are known to have been acted, is the New Inn at Gloucester.

There are many examples of the great hall: in the colleges at Oxford and Cambridge, the Halls of the Inns of Court in London, Hampton Court, and elsewhere. They are all of a pattern. At one end is the dais where the more illustrious sit; at the other the 'screens' through which are two doors leading to the kitchens beneath the 'minstrels' gallery'. With this screen as background, the players acted, using both doors and gallery as part of their stage. (See illustration facing p. 96.)

In the playhouse the seating arrangements of inns and the form of the stage of the great hall were combined.

The Theatre, as has been seen, was built in 1576, and the Globe in 1599. When Henslowe and Alleyn decided to build the Fortune in 1600 they employed the builder of the Globe, and drew up a detailed and elaborate agreement. It is so important a document of stage history that it is worth reproducing in full:

THIS INDENTURE made the eighth day of January, 1599 [1600], and in the two and fortieth year of the reign of our sovereign Lady Elizabeth, by the grace of God Queen of England, France and Ireland, defender of the faith, &c., Between Phillip Henslowe and Edward Alleyn of the parish of Saint Saviours in Southwark, in the county of Surrey, gentlemen, on the one part, And Peter Street, citizen and carpenter of London, on the other part, WITNESSETH that, whereas the said Phillip Henslowe and Edward Alleyn the day of the date hereof have bargained, compounded and agreed with the said Peter Street for the erecting, building, and setting up of a new house and stage for a playhouse, in and upon a certain plot or parcel of ground appointed out for that purpose, situate and being near Golding Lane in the parish of Saint Giles without Cripplegate of London To be by him the said Peter Street, or some other sufficient workmen of his providing and appointment, and at his proper costs and charges, for the consideration hereafter in these presents expressed, made, erected, builded and set up, in manner and form following; that is to say,

The frame of the said house to be set square, and to contain fourscore foot of lawful assize every way square without, and fifty-five foot of like assize square every way within, with a good, sure, and strong foundation of piles, brick, lime, and sand, both without and within, to be wrought one foot of assize at the least above the ground.

And the said frame to contain three stories in height. The first or lower story to contain twelve foot of lawful assize in height, the second story eleven foot of lawful assize in height, And the third or upper story to contain nine foot of lawful assize in height.

All which stories shall contain twelve foot and a half of lawful assize in breadth throughout, besides a jutty forwards in either of the said two upper stories of ten inches of lawful assize, with four convenient divisions for gentlemen's rooms, and other sufficient and convenient divisions for twopenny rooms, with necessary seats to be placed and set as well in these rooms as throughout all the rest of the galleries of the said house; and with such like stairs, conveyances, and divisions, without and within, as are made and contrived in and to the late erected playhouse on the Bank, in the said parish of Saint Saviours, called the Globe;

With a Stage and Tiring-house to be made, erected and set up within the said frame, with a shadow or cover over the said stage, which stage shall be placed and set, as also the staircases of the said frame, in such sort as is prefigured in a plot thereof drawn,

And which stage shall contain in length forty and three foot of lawful assize, and in breadth to extend to the middle of the yard of the said house,

The same stage to be paled in below with good strong and sufficient new oaken boards,

And likewise the lower story of the said frame withinside, and the same lower story to be also laid over and fenced with strong iron pikes,

And the said stage to be in all other proportions contrived and fashioned like unto the stage of the said playhouse called the

Globe; with convenient windows and lights glazed to the said tiring-house,

And the said frame, stage and staircases to be covered with tile, and to have a sufficient gutter of lead, to carry and convey the water from the covering of the said stage to fall backwards,

And also all the said frame and the staircases thereof to be sufficiently enclosed without with lath, lime and hair, and the gentlemen's rooms and twopenny rooms to be sealed with lath, lime and hair; and all the floors of the said galleries, stories and stage to be boarded with good and sufficient new deal boards of the whole thickness, where need shall be.

And the said house, and other things before mentioned to be made and done, to be in all other contrivitions, conveyances, fashions, thing and things, effected, finished, and done according to the manner and fashion of the said house called the Globe.

Saving only that all the principal and main posts of the said frame and stage forward, shall be square and wrought pilaster-wise, with carved proportions called Satyrs to be placed and set on top of every of the same posts.

And saving also that the said Peter Street shall not be charged with any manner of painting in or about the said frame, house, or stage, or any part thereof, nor rendering the walls within nor ceiling any more or other rooms than the gentlemen's rooms, twopenny rooms and stage, before remembered.

Now THEREUPON the said Peter Street doth covenant, promise and grant for himself, his executors and administrators, to and with the said Phillip Henslowe and Edward Alleyn, and either of them and the executors and administrators of them, and either of them by these presents, in manner and form following, that is to say,

That he the said Peter Street, his executors or assigns, shall and will, at his or their own proper costs and charges, well, workmanlike and substantially make, erect, set up and fully finish in and by all things, according to the true meaning of these presents, with good, strong, and substantial new timber and other necessary stuff,

All the said frame and other works whatsoever in and upon the said plot or parcel of ground (being not by any authority restrained, and having ingress, egress and regress to do the same) before the five and twentieth day of July next coming after the date hereof;

AND SHALL ALSO at his or their like costs and charges, provide and find all manner of workmen, timber, joists, rafters, boards, doors, bolts, hinges, brick, tile, lath, lime, hair, sand, nails, lead, iron, glass, workmanship and other things whatsoever, which shall be needful, convenient and necessary for the said frame and works and every part thereof,

And shall also make all the said frame in every point for scantlings larger and bigger in assize than the scantlings of the timber of the said new erected house called the Globe.

AND ALSO that he the said Peter Street shall forthwith, as well by himself as by such other and so many workmen as shall be convenient and necessary, enter into and upon the said buildings and works,

And shall in reasonable manner proceed therein, without any wilful detraction until the same shall be fully effected and finished.

IN CONSIDERATION of all which buildings, and of all stuff and workmanship hereto belonging,

The said Phillip Henslowe and Edward Alleyn, and either of them, for themselves, their and either of their executors and administrators, do jointly and severally covenant to grant to and with the said Peter Street, his executors and administrators, by these presents,

That they, the said Phillip Henslowe and Edward Alleyn, or one of them or the executors, administrators or assigns of them or one of them, shall and will well and truly pay or cause to be paid unto the said Peter Street, his executors or assigns, at the place aforesaid appointed for the erecting of the said frame, The full sum of four hundred and forty pounds of lawful money of England, in manner and form following, that is to say, At such time And when as the timber work of the said frame shall be raised and set up by the said Peter Street, his executors or assigns, or within seven days then next following, two hundred and twenty pounds,

And at such time and when as the said frame and work shall be fully effected and finished as is aforesaid, or within seven days then next following, the other two hundred and twenty pounds, without fraud or covin.

PROVIDED ALWAYS, and it is agreed between the said parties, That whatsoever sum or sums of money the said Phillip Henslowe and Edward Alleyn, or either of them, or the executors or assigns of them or either of them shall lend or deliver unto the said Peter Street, his executors or assigns or any other by his appointment or consent, for or concerning the said works or any part thereof, or any stuff thereto belonging, before the raising and setting up of the said frame, shall be reputed, accepted, taken and accounted in part of the first payment aforesaid of the said sum of four hundred and forty pounds;

And all such sum and sums of money as they, or any of them, shall as aforesaid lend or deliver between the raising of the said frame and finishing thereof, and of all the rest of the said works, shall be reputed, accepted, taken and accounted in part of the last payment aforesaid of the same sum of four hundred and forty pounds; anything above said to the contrary not withstanding.

IN WITNESS WHEREOF the parties abovesaid to these present indentures interchangeably have set their hands and seals. Given the day and year first above-written.*

It is not always remembered that the Elizabethan playhouse was very small. The external dimensions of the theatre measured 80 by 80 feet; and of the interior area of 55 feet by 55, the stage occupied almost half. Henslowe's Fortune was square, but the pictures which remain of the outside of other theatres show that they were circular or octagonal. Within there were three tiers of galleries look-

Henslowe Papers, edited by W. W. Greg, p. 4.

ing down upon the yard or pit where the poorer spectators stood, or possibly sat on stools. The stage itself,
which is technically called an 'apron stage', jutted out
into the yard, so that when the house was crowded the
players were surrounded on three sides. Over the stage

THE EXTERIOR OF THE GLOBE
PLAYHOUSE, FROM VISSCHER'S
VIEW OF LONDON, 1616

there was a 'shadow' or roof which protected the players
from the rain. At the back of the stage on either side there
were two entrances by side doors. By these the characters
entered and disappeared. It was a convenient arrangement, leading to some easy symbolism. When two nations

were at war, one side is England and the other France. When a procession passes over the stage, it enters at one door and goes out by the other.

The recess at the back of the stage underneath the balcony was known as the 'tiring-house' or 'the place behind the stage'. Usually it was curtained off, but when the curtains were drawn it provided a convenient inner stage for a variety of purposes — tombs, caves, studies, bedrooms. The inner stage was much used, especially for set scenes such as taverns, or bedrooms. There was no general curtain concealing the whole stage, so that all scenes on the main stage began with an entrance and ended with an exit. In tragedies, unless the dead died within the curtains, a funeral procession gave a fitting close.

Over the back of the stage, parallel with the second gallery or indeed part of it, there was an upper stage. This also was, when not required, covered with a curtain. In front jutted out a balcony which was used to represent the walls of a town. It served, for instance, as the walls of Flint Castle where King Richard II addressed Bolingbroke below. In *King John* it was the wall of Angers whence the citizens addressed the two kings and later the prison wall from which little Arthur leaps down to his death.

The upper inner stage was the same size as the recess and could be used as a bed chamber or for any other purpose when the dramatist required an upper level. It was Cleopatra's monument whither the dying Antony was hoisted up. On either side of the chamber were windows.

The stage directions of the early editions of plays are

THE GLOBE THEATRE: WOOD-ENGRAVING BY
R. J. BEEDHAM AFTER A RECONSTRUCTION BY
DR J. C. ADAMS

THE HALL OF THE MIDDLE TEMPLE
(From the dais)

usually scant and formal, but at times they will indicate the production.

There are two early Quartos of *Romeo & Juliet*, and both contain illuminating stage directions (shown in italics) which show how the play was produced.* In Act I, Scene iv, Benvolio, Mercutio, and Romeo are on their way to the feast at Capulet's house. After some talk *They march about the stage, and serving men come forth with napkins*. The walk indicates that they are going, and the serving men that they have arrived at the feast. The serving men speak to each other, and then *Enter all the guests and gentlewomen to the Maskers*. Capulet welcomes them: *Music plays and they dance*.

The directions in Act III, Scene v, show how the upper stage was used. Romeo has spent the night with Juliet. The scene begins with *Enter Romeo and Juliet at the window*. Romeo gives her a farewell kiss. *He goeth down*. When he has made his exit, Juliet addresses fickle Fortune, then *She goeth down from the window: Enter Lady Capulet* — on the main upper stage.

The episode (Act IV, Scenes ii–v) where Juliet takes the sleeping potion shows how upper stage and recess were sometimes used in combination. At the beginning of Scene ii, Capulet has declared that Juliet shall be married to Count Paris; Juliet has gone to consult the friar. The scene opens with *Enter Father Capulet, mother, nurse, and serving men two or three*. Juliet enters through the curtain of the inner stage and tells her father that she will no

*It is perhaps unnecessary to warn the reader that the reconstruction of the action of *Romeo and Juliet* is largely conjecture.

longer oppose him. Juliet and the Nurse go out through the curtain of the recess, Capulet and the rest by one of the doors.

Scene iii. The curtains of the upper stage are opened revealing Juliet and the Nurse laying clothes on the bed. Lady Capulet enters and goes out with the Nurse. Juliet takes the potion; *she falls upon her bed within the curtains.* The curtains of the upper stage are closed.

Scene iv. The curtains of the inner stage are opened. The stage has now become the hall of the Capulets' house. Lady Capulet enters with the Nurse *with herbs.* Capulet enters. Lady Capulet and the Nurse go out. Preparations for the wedding are going forward; these are indicated by – *Enter three or four with spits, and logs, and baskets* – who pass across the stage. Music is played. Capulet calls to the Nurse who comes in. He orders her to call the bride:

> Go waken Juliet, go and trim her up,
> I'll go and chat with Paris, hie, make haste,
> Make haste, the bridegroom, he is come already,
> Make haste I say.   [*Exit.*

No exit is marked for the Nurse. She goes up to the upper stage by the stairs at the back of the recess and from within opens the curtains of the upper stage, thereby revealing Juliet lying on her bed. She tries to awaken Juliet and at her cries Lady Capulet followed by old Capulet go up the stairs and appear on the upper stage. The Friar and the Count enter the upper stage. After their lamentations, *they all but the Nurse go forth casting rosemary on her and shutting the curtains of the upper stage.* The action then continues on the main stage until the end.

In the last scene the stage directions are – *Enter* [by one of the doors] *Count Paris and his page with flowers and sweet water* . . . *Paris strews the tomb* [i.e. the other door] *with flowers* . . . *The Page whistles and calls: My Lord* . . . *Enter Romeo and his man Balthasar with a torch, mattock, and a crow of iron* . . . *Romeo opens the tomb* [i.e. the door]. Paris comes forward and encounters him. *They fight* . . . *Exit the Page* . . . Paris *Dies* . . . Romeo then enters the open door. The curtains of the inner stage are opened, and Romeo appears within the 'tomb':

> For here lies Juliet, and her beauty makes
> This vault a feasting presence full of light.

He takes the poison and *Falls* . . . *Enter Friar* [by a door] *with a lantern, crow, and spade* . . . *Friar stoops and looks on the blood and weapons* . . . *Juliet rises* . . . *Exit Friar Laurence* . . . *Enter Boy and Watch* . . . Juliet hears them approaching. *She stabs herself and falls* – by the bier over Romeo's body. *Enter Romeo's man* . . . *Enter Friar and another Watchman* . . . *Enter the Prince* . . . *Enter Capulet and his Wife* . . . *Enter Montague* . . . The sorrowing parents behold the tragedy of the lovers. Then the Prince says –

> Seal up the mouth of outrage for a while.

At these words the curtains of the inner stage are drawn together, and the story is brought effectively to its close with the two fathers reconciled before the curtain which now conceals the bodies of the dead lovers.

The structure of the stage considerably affected plays. On the apron stage the actor came forward right into the midst of his audience, and was therefore in the closest possible touch. He was not, as in the modern theatre, divided from them by a curtain or by light and darkness. Hence the device of soliloquy was perfectly natural. The actor explains his position and his thoughts to those who are immediately in front of him. Moreover he was so close that there was no need for him to shout, so that the greatest subtlety of voice, gesture, and expression was possible.

There was apparently no scenery, and plays were acted in daylight. The Elizabethan actor was thus without the effects produced on the modern stage by lighting, scenery – realistic or symbolic – and elaborate orchestral effects. In their place he gained his effects by a direct assault on the emotions and the imagination of the spectators. Poetry was a natural medium for dramatic speech, especially at exalted moments, and a good actor could carry his audience with him by the emotional effect of rhetoric.

A scene ended when all the actors had gone off the stage and a new set of characters came on. There was thus a quick continuity of performance with no break in the illusion. As there was no scenery, so there was no limit to the number of scenes. Usually the exact locality of the scene was unimportant. When it was necessary, Shakespeare showed it in the dialogue.

'What country, friends, is this?' Viola asks.

'This is Illyria, lady,' the sea captain answers.

But for the most part a simple property or garment was sufficient. Chairs or stools showed indoor scenes; a man wearing riding-boots was a messenger; a king wearing his armour was on the field of battle; a watchman carrying a lantern indicated the streets of a city at night. The most important difference between the modern and the Elizabethan theatre is that Elizabethan plays were all acted by daylight.

Such arrangements are simple, but not crude. All drama implies an acceptance of conventions and a use of the imagination, and properties can easily replace scenery. The properties were many and varied. Amongst the Henslowe *Papers* is a complete inventory of the properties belonging to the Admiral's Company in 1598:

i rock, i cage, i tomb, i Hell mouth.
i tomb of Guido, i tomb of Dido, i bedstead.
viii lances, i pair of stairs for Phaeton.
ii steeples, & i chime of bells, & i beacon.
i heifer for the play of Phaeton, the limbs dead.
i globe, & i golden sceptre; iii clubs.
ii marchpanes, & the City of Rome.
i golden fleece; ii rackets; i bay tree.
i wooden hatchet; i leather hatchet.
i wooden canopy; old Mahomet's head.
i lion skin; i bear's skin; & Phaeton's limbs & Phaeton's chariot; & Argus' head.
Neptune's fork and garland.
i 'crosers' staff; Kent's wooden leg.
Iris head, & rainbow; i little altar.
viii vizards; Tamberlain's bridle; i wooden mattock.
Cupid's bow, & quiver; the cloth of the Sun & Moon.
i boar's head & Cerberus' iii heads.
i Caduceus; ii moss banks, & i snake.
ii fanes of feathers; Bellendon stable; i tree of golden apples; Tantalus' tree, ix iron targets.
i copper target, & xvii foils.
iiii wooden targets; i greeve armour.
i sign for Mother Redcap; i buckler.

Mercury's wings; Tasso's picture; i helmet with a dragon;
    i shield, with iii lions; i elm bowl.
i chain of dragons; i gilt spear.
ii coffins; i bull's head; and i 'vylter'.
iii timbrels; i dragon in Faustus.
i lion; ii lions heads; i great horse with his legs; i sackbut.
i wheel and frame in the Siege of London.
i pair of wrought gloves.
i Pope's mitre.
iii Imperial crowns; i plain crown.
i ghost's crown; i crown with a sun.
i frame for the heading in Black Joan.
i black dog.
i cauldron for the Jew.*

[This list is reproduced in modern spelling. Henslowe's spelling was erratic and individual, and some of the interpretations
are questionable. It is not known how 'Hell mouth' or the 'City
of Rome' were represented as properties. Of the others, a
'marchpane' was an elaborate marzipan cake; the 'frame for the
heading' was a piece of stage machinery to produce the illusion
of a beheading.]

There was some attempt at realistic presentation. When
characters were stabbed they bled, as Caesar is made to
bleed in *Julius Caesar*. In the play of *Arden of Feversham*
there was a fog, which must have been represented somehow. The stage machinery was, however, crude and irri-
tating to the artistic sense of Ben Jonson, who sneered at
it in the prologue to *Every Man in his Humour*:

> He rather prays you will be pleased to see
> One such to-day, as other plays should be;
> Where neither chorus wafts you o'er the seas,
> Nor creaking throne comes down the boys to please;

Henslowe Papers, p. 116.

Nor nimble squib is seen to make afeard
The gentlewomen; nor rolled bullet heard
To say, it thunders; nor tempestuous drum
Rumbles, to tell you when the storm doth come.

On the other hand costumes were sometimes lavish and imposing. When the Admiral's Men produced a play of Cardinal Wolsey in 1601 they bought 'two pile velvet of carnadine at twenty shillings a yard, satins at twelve shillings and taffetas at twelve and six.' The bill for material alone came to £21 in money of the day.

There was an elaborate system of trumpet calls; sennets, tuckets, alarums, retreats, flourishes, appear frequently in stage directions. No king enters or goes out without a flourish. On the modern stage these trumpet calls are usually half-hearted; on the Elizabethan they had a considerable psychological effect. The stage directions, especially of some plays produced at the Rose Theatre, show that the stage carpenter was ambitious.

*Let there be a brazen head set in the middle of the place behind the
    Stage, out of which cast flames of fire, drums rumble within:
    Enter two Priests.*

*Exit Venus; or if you conveniently can, let a chair come down from
    the top of the stage and draw her up.*

*The Magi with their rods beat the ground, and from under the same
    riseth a brave arbour; the King returneth in another suit, while
    the Trumpets sound.*

*Upon this prayer she departeth, and a flame of fire appeareth from
    beneath, and Radagon is swallowed.*

Jonas the Prophet cast out of the Whale's belly upon the stage.

Plays at the Rose Theatre were acted on the repertory system. The Company kept a considerable range of plays available and played a different play each afternoon. The average life of a new play was about ten performances. Popular plays were acted more often, but the less successful sometimes disappeared after the second or third performance. Continuous runs were unknown. Thus a typical fortnight – 1–14 February 1596 – shows that the Admiral's Men played the following plays:

> *The Jew of Malta.*
> *First part of Fortunatus.*
> *The Wise Men of Westchester.*
> *Longshanks.*
> *Harry the Fifth.*
> *Crack me these Nuts.*
> *Pythagoras.*
> *Fortunatus.*
> *Chinon of England.*
> *The Blind Beggar of Alexandria.*
> *Dr Faustus.*
> *Pythagoras.*

Thus on twelve acting days ten different plays were acted. Of these one – *The Blind Beggar of Alexandria* – was a new play, and six no longer survive. A large proportion of Elizabethan plays have perished.

It follows that the Elizabethan actor was a busy man, constantly rehearsing new plays. He had little time for long, elaborate, and exhausting preparations; but he belonged to a team and the trained actor was ready in emergency to improvise, and indeed Italian actors at this time were so clever that, given a story, they could make up the play as they went along.

The Elizabethan acting company was a 'fellowship of players', and they worked on the share system. The actors were partners in the concern, and therefore the company remained constant. There were ten to fifteen regular sharers, and in addition some hired men and boys learning the business who ultimately might rise to be sharers.

Amongst Henslowe's papers there is an agreement between Henslowe and Jacob Meade with an actor named Robert Dawes. Dawes agrees for a space of three years to play with such company as Phillip Henslowe and Jacob Meade shall agree; 'at the rate of one whole share according to the custom of the players; and that he the said Robert Dawes shall and will at all times during the said term duly attend all such rehearsal which shall the night before the rehearsal be given publicly out; and if that he the said Robert Dawes shall at any time fail to come at the hour appointed, then he shall and will pay to the said Phillip Henslowe and Jacob Meade their executors or assigns twelve pence; and that if he come not before the said rehearsal is ended then the said Robert Dawes is contented to pay two shillings; and further that if the said Robert Dawes shall not every day whereon any play is or ought to be played be ready apparelled and . . . to begin the play at the hour of three of the clock in the afternoon unless by six of the same company he shall be licensed to the contrary, that then he the said Robert Dawes shall and will pay unto the said Phillip and Jacob or their assigns three shillings, and that if he the said Robert Dawes happen to be overcome with drink at the time when he ought to play, by the judgement of four of the said company, he shall and will pay ten shillings and if he the said Robert Dawes shall fail to come during any play having no license or just excuse of sickness he is contented to pay twenty shillings.'

The agreement then proceeds to discuss the problem of wearing-apparel and adds the clause that if Dawes 'shall at any time after the play is ended depart or go out of the house with any of their apparel on his body or if the said Robert Dawes shall carry away any property belonging to the said company, or shall be consenting or privy to any other of the said company going out of the house with any of their apparel on his or their bodies, he the said Robert Dawes shall and will forfeit and pay unto the said Phillip and Jacob or their administrators or assigns the sum of forty pounds of lawful money of England.'

The importance of the company system is considerable. Nowadays a producer will assemble actors suitable for a particular play, and he can draw from a vast reservoir of all kinds and types. If he needs an actor who specializes in taking the part of a chimpanzee, he will find several available. Shakespeare had to write for his company as it existed. He could not therefore produce characters for which the company had no physical representative. On the other hand he made use of the peculiarities of the actors, and it is noticeable how certain physical types recur. In the company there was a tall man with a thin hatchet face; another who specialized in 'silly gentleman' parts. Richard Burbage, the chief tragedian, matures. There were no young Romeos as a chief character in Shakespeare's later plays. Instead his heroes are mature men: Othello, Lear, Prospero. The changes are not less noticeable in the girls' parts. No women actresses appeared in Shakespeare's time – nor indeed until the Restoration – and women's parts were taken by boys. The boy actor is not necessarily a disadvantage. As boys could only act women's parts until their voices broke, Shakespeare was spared Rosalinds and Violas of forty. There were not more than two or three boys at once, and therefore not many women in any one play.

CHAPTER VI

The Shakespeare Canon

In any study of the development of Shakespeare's art it is necessary first to discover the date when each play was written. This is not so easy. So few of the necessary records survive that it is seldom possible to date any Elizabethan play exactly. Plays acted by the companies which played in Henslowe's theatres are recorded in his diary, which gives either the date of the first performance, or else details of the payments made to dramatists. But only a small proportion of the plays written during Shakespeare's lifetime were acted at the Rose or Fortune Playhouses; for the other companies and playhouses there is no record comparable to the *Diary*.

Shakespeare's plays must therefore be dated by argument, and deduction from such evidence as can be collected. This is of three kinds: (*a*) external; (*b*) internal; (*c*) style. By combining all kinds of evidence the canon of the plays has been worked out, and there is general agreement on the approximate dates at which most of the plays were written.

The most valuable kind of evidence is external, that is, a clear mention or reference to a particular play. There are many of these references. Thus in *Gesta Grayorum*, an account of the famous 'Gray's Inn Revels' of 1594–5, there is a note that:

on the night of the 28th December, 1594, after dancing and revelling with gentlewomen, a 'Comedy of Errors' (like to Plautus his 'Menechmus') was played by the players.

A German traveller named Platter who visited London in 1599 noted in his diary that:

After dinner on the 21st of September, at about two o'clock, I went with my companions over the water, and in the strewn roof-house [i.e. playhouse with a thatched roof] saw the tragedy of the first Emperor Julius with at least fifteen characters very well acted. At the end of the comedy they danced according to their custom with extreme elegance. Two in men's clothes and two in women's gave this performance, in wonderful combination with each other.*

John Manningham, a Barrister of the Middle Temple, recorded in his diary under the date 2 February 1602:

At our feast we had a play called 'Twelfth Night, or What you Will,' much like the Comedy of Errors, or Menechmi in Plautus, but most like and near to that in Italian called *Inganni*. A good practice in it to make the Steward believe his Lady widow was in love with him, by counterfeiting a letter as from his Lady in general terms, telling him what she liked best in him, and prescribing his gesture in smiling, his apparel, etc., and then when he came to practise making believe they took him to be mad.

The 'Revels Accounts' of the Court show that payments were made in 1604–5 for a performance of *Othello* before King James I and his Court on 1 November, on 4

*E. K. Chambers: *The Elizabethan Stage*, ii, pp. 364–5.

November for *The Merry Wives of Windsor*, and 26 December for *Measure for Measure*; in January for *Love's Labour's Lost*, on 7 January for *Henry V*, and on 10 February for *The Merchant of Venice*, which so pleased King James that he commanded a second performance on the 12th. Later, payments were made for *The Tempest*, acted before the King on 1 November 1611, and again in February 1613, at the marriage festivities of the Princess Elizabeth.

Valuable evidence for the dates of the earlier plays is given in Francis Meres' list of a dozen quoted on p. 13. These plays at least were produced before Meres' book went to press in the summer of 1598. Moreover it is probable that other plays, more important, had not then been produced, otherwise Meres would hardly have failed to mention *Hamlet*, *Othello*, and *Lear*.

Such evidence as this seldom gives the date of the first performance of any play, but it certainly shows that the play had been written before a certain date.

The second kind of evidence is internal, where in the play itself there is some unmistakable reference to an identifiable event. There are not many of these in Shakespeare's plays, for although he often reminded his audience of current events in some significant speech, he seldom makes a direct reference.

There is, however, a clear reference to the triumphant departure, on 27 March 1599, of the Earl of Essex for Ireland in the *Chorus* before Act V of *Henry V*:

> But now behold,
> In the quick forge and working-house of thought,
> How London doth pour out her citizens,

> The Mayor and all his brethren in best sort,
> Like to the Senators of th'antique Rome,
> With the plebeians swarming at their heels,
> Go forth and fetch their conquering Caesar in:
> As by a lower, but by loving likelihood,
> Were now the General of our gracious Empress,
> As in good time he may, from Ireland coming,
> Bringing rebellion broached on his sword;
> How many would the peaceful City quit,
> To welcome him?

As Essex failed utterly and returned secretly to London on 28 September, it follows that the *Chorus* was written soon after March 1599.

In *Hamlet* there is a clear reference to the wars of the theatres in 1600–1 in Hamlet's remarks:

HAMLET: What players are they?

ROSENCRANTZ: Even those you were wont to take delight in, the tragedians of the City.

HAMLET: How chances it they travel? their residence both in reputation and profit was better both ways.

ROSENCRANTZ: I think their inhibition comes by the means of the late innovation.

HAMLET: Do they hold the same estimation they did when I was in the City? are they so follow'd?

ROSENCRANTZ: No indeed, they are not.

HAMLET: How comes it? do they grow rusty?

ROSENCRANTZ: Nay, their endeavour keeps in the wonted pace; but there is sir an aery of children, little eyases, that cry out on the top of question; and are most tyrannically clapp'd for't: these are now the fashion, and so berattle the common Stages (so they call them) that many wearing rapiers, are afraid of goose-quills, and dare scarce come thither.

HAMLET: What, are they children? who maintains 'em? how are they escoted? Will they pursue the quality no longer than they can sing? will they not say afterwards if they should grow themselves to common Players (as it is most like if their means are no better) their writers do them wrong, to make them exclaim against their own succession?

ROSENCRANTZ: Faith there has been much to do on both sides: and the nation holds it no sin, to tarre them to controversy. There was for a while, no money bid for argument, unless the Poet and the Player went to cuffs in the question.

HAMLET: Is't possible?

GUILDENSTERN: O there has been much throwing about of brains.

HAMLET: Do the Boys carry it away?

ROSENCRANTZ: Ay that they do my Lord, Hercules and his load too.

The third method of dating, by style, is not so exact. Nevertheless the changes and developments of Shakespeare's poetic style are so noticeable that a play can be reasonably placed by style alone in one of four groups – early, mature, concentrated, and late. By a combination of the three methods the plays can be dated approximately, and roughly in the order of writing, so that it is possible not only to trace Shakespeare's development but also to see his plays against the background of his times.

Lear, for instance, was apparently written in 1606. It must have been written before the Christmas of that year, because on the 26 November 1607, Nathaniel Butter and John Busby entered in the Stationers' Register:

A book called Master William Shakespeare his history of King Lear, as it was played before the King's Majesty at Whitehall upon Saint Stephen's night at Christmas last, by his majesty's servants playing usually at the Globe on the Bankside.

The play was thus acted at the Court in the Christmas holidays of 1606. The earliest date for its writing was 1603. Edgar, disguised as 'Poor Tom, the Bedlam beggar', mutters:

> . . . five fiends have been in poor Tom at once; of lust, as Obidicut, Hobbididance Prince of dumbness, Mahu of stealing, Modo of murder, Flibbertigibbet of mopping and mowing, who since possesses chambermaids and waiting women.

These names Shakespeare took from a book called *A declaration of egregious popish impostures* which was written by the Rev. Samuel Harsnett, Chaplain to the Bishop of London, and published early in 1603.

It is possible to get nearer. In the play, Gloucester, who was a believer in omens and portents, says to Edgar:

> These late eclipses in the sun and moon portend no good to us: though the wisdom of Nature can reason it thus, and thus, yet Nature finds itself scourg'd by the sequent effects. Love cools, friendship falls off, brothers divide. In cities, mutinies; in countries, discord; in palaces, treason; and the bond crack'd, 'twixt son and father. This villain of mine comes under the prediction; there's son against father; the King falls from bias of Nature, there's father against child. We have seen the best of our time. Machinations, hollowness, treachery, and all ruinous disorders follow us disquietly to our graves.

A little later Edmund, speaking to Edgar, cynically echoes Gloucester's words:

> I am thinking, brother, of a prediction I read this other day,

what should follow these eclipses. . . . I promise you, the effects he writes of, succeed unhappily, as of unnaturalness between the child and the parent, death, dearth, dissolutions of ancient amities, divisions in state, menaces and maledictions against King and nobles, needless diffidences, banishment of friends, dissipation of cohorts, nuptial breaches, and I know not what.

Shakespeare took these speeches from a little pamphlet called *Strange, fearful and true news which happened at Carlstadt in the Kingdom of Croatia*. It was translated from the High Dutch and told of terrible signs and portents which (according to the editor, one Edward Gresham, an almanack maker) were divine portents of threatening disaster:

The Earth's and Moon's late and horrible obscurations, the frequent eclipsations of the fixed bodies; by the wandering, the fixed stars, I mean the planets, within these few years more than ordinary, shall without doubt (salved divine inhibition) have their effects no less admirable, than the positions unusual. Which PEUCER with many more too long to rehearse out of continual observation and the consent of all authors noted to be, new leagues, traitorous designments, catching at kingdoms, translation of empire, downfall of men in authority, emulations, ambition, innovations, factious sects, schisms and much disturbance and troubles in religion and matters of the Church, with many other things infallible in sequent such orbical positions and phenomenes.

The preface to this work is dated 11 February 1606. It follows that *Lear* was written between this date and its performance in the Christmas of the same year. The style, too, of the play, with its concentrated and pregnant imagery, shows that it was written about the same time as

Macbeth and after *Hamlet* and *Othello*. There is some definite evidence for assigning *Macbeth* also to the same year, 1606.

The full list of Shakespeare's plays with their approximate dates is as follows:

	PLAYS		FIRST PRINTED
1591.	HENRY VI *three parts* . . .		*Folio* [1623]
	RICHARD III		1597
	TITUS ANDRONICUS		1594
	LOVE'S LABOUR'S LOST . . .		1598
	THE TWO GENTLEMEN OF VERONA	.	*Folio*
	THE COMEDY OF ERRORS . .	.	*Folio*
	THE TAMING OF THE SHREW .	.	*Folio*
1594.	ROMEO AND JULIET .	(*pirated* 1597)	1599
	A MIDSUMMER NIGHT'S DREAM .	.	1600
	RICHARD II	.	1597
	KING JOHN	.	*Folio*
	THE MERCHANT OF VENICE .	.	1600
1597.	HENRY IV *part i* . . .	.	1598
	HENRY IV *part ii* . . .	.	1600
	MUCH ADO ABOUT NOTHING .	.	1600
	MERRY WIVES OF WINDSOR	(*pirated* 1602)	*Folio*
	AS YOU LIKE IT . . .	.	*Folio*
	JULIUS CAESAR . . .	.	*Folio*
	HENRY V . . .	(*pirated* 1600)	*Folio*
	TROILUS AND CRESSIDA .	.	1609
1601.	HAMLET	(*pirated* 1603)	1604
	TWELFTH NIGHT . . .	.	*Folio*
	MEASURE FOR MEASURE . .	.	*Folio*
	ALL'S WELL THAT ENDS WELL .	.	*Folio*
	OTHELLO	.	1622
1606.	LEAR	.	1608
	MACBETH	.	*Folio*
	TIMON OF ATHENS . . .	.	*Folio*
	ANTONY AND CLEOPATRA .	.	*Folio*
	CORIOLANUS . . .	.	*Folio*
1609.	PERICLES . .	(*omitted from the Folio*)	1609
1611.	CYMBELINE . . .	.	*Folio*

PLAYS FIRST PRINTED

1611	THE WINTER'S TALE	.	.	.	.	*Folio*
	THE TEMPEST	.	.	.	.	*Folio*
	HENRY VIII	.	.	.	.	*Folio*

CHAPTER VII

Development of Shakespeare's Style

WHEN Shakespeare began to write for the stage the standard of acting was set by Edward Alleyn, and of plays by those who wrote for him, especially Marlowe, Greene, and Kyd. Alleyn's most popular plays were Marlowe's *Tamburlaine* and *Jew of Malta*, Greene's *Orlando Furioso* and *Friar Bacon*, and Kyd's *Spanish Tragedy*. All had much in common, and at first Shakespeare imitated the common style and mannerisms so closely that some critics argue hotly whether he was indeed the sole author of some of the early plays attributed to him in the First Folio.

Audiences in the early 1590s were still unsophisticated, simple in their demands, and hearty in their appetites. They expected characters on the stage to talk in high-sounding phrases and to make long speeches on every occasion, full of rhetorical devices, stuffed with mythology and bookish similes. Thus Marlowe, wishing to express the perplexities of Zenocrate, torn between affection for her father and her former lover, and her new love for Tamburlaine, is made to say:

> Now shame and duty, love and fear presents
> A thousand sorrows to my martyred soul.
> Whom should I wish the fatal victory,
> When my poor pleasures are divided thus,
> And racked by duty from my cursed heart?
> My father and my first betrothed love

Must fight against my life and present love;
Wherein the change I use condemns my faith,
And makes my deeds infamous through the world.
But as the gods, to end the Trojan's toil,
Prevented Turnus of Lavinia,
And fatally enriched Aeneas' love,
So, for a final issue to my griefs,
To pacify my country and my love,
Must Tamburlaine by their resistless powers,
With virtue of a gentle victory,
Conclude a league of honour to my hope;
Then, as the powers divine have pre-ordained,
With happy safety of my father's life
Send like defence of fair Arabia.

This is the language of the literary student who turns naturally to Virgil for an apt parallel in Turnus and Aeneas, pleasing to those who had also read the *Aeneid* but quite inappropriate to the distressed Egyptian damsel.

Marlowe was more successful in writing blank verse than the others, but even he could not keep a kind of shuttle rhythm out of his lines. He did not attempt to write blank verse as in any way representing normal speech: his aim was to be gorgeous and magnificent, to write in 'high astounding terms' which suited the style of Alleyn and his company, who liked sound and fury.

At first Shakespeare admired the current fashions. He revelled in mere words, their sound, colour, and glitter. He was at his best in Comedy and he liked rhyme, for he often moved more freely within the restraints of rhyme than in the freer blank verse. Comedy was still his natural outlet. It gave him the chance of choosing words and phrases with an ease and subtlety which, though this kind of cleverness has long passed out of fashion, no one else ever touched. It is shown at its best in *Love's Labour's Lost* in such a speech as the defence of 'barbarism' which he gave to Berowne, a bubbling, many-coloured cascade of words. The thought is simple: that those who neglect everything for the sake of learning and never fall in love, miss more than they gain by their studies. In this speech he takes up the idea of light and darkness, to juggle with them in a dazzling display of verbal trickery:

> Why! all delights are vain, and that most vain
> Which with pain purchas'd, doth inherit pain,
> As painfully to pore upon a book,
>> To seek the light of truth, while truth the while
> Doth falsely blind the eyesight of his look:
>> Light, seeking light, doth light of light beguile:
> So ere you find where light in darkness lies,
> Your light grows dark by losing of your eyes.
> Study me how to please the eye indeed,
>> By fixing it upon a fairer eye,
> Who dazzling so, that eye shall be his heed,
>> And give him light that it was blinded by.
> Study is like the heaven's glorious Sun,
>> That will not be deep-search'd with saucy looks:
> Small have continual plodders ever won,
>> Save base authority from others' books.
> These earthly godfathers of heaven's lights,
>> That give a name to every fixed star,
> Have no more profit of their shining nights,
>> Than those that walk and wot not what they are.
> Too much to know, is to know nought but fame:
> And every godfather can give a name.

The four-fold 'light', each with a slightly different meaning, in

> Light, seeking light, doth light of light beguile,

is an amazingly clever trick.

The outburst is neither profound thought nor good drama, for everything must stand still until Berowne has finished. It is the sheer exuberance of an athlete who has discovered that he can play what game he likes with words. Yet the speech itself is significant. It is the answer of the 'upstart crow' whose Latin was little and Greek less to those intellectual snobs who believed that all learning lived in books. Shakespeare's lack of book-learning was a blessing. When he needed a simile or an image he found it in his own experience and not in his reading.

In his early tragedies Shakespeare was less successful. He was still inclined to be heavy, especially when he wrote for effect. In *Richard III* Tyrrell describes the death of the little princes – an occasion for pathos and sentimentality:

> The tyrannous and bloody act is done;
> The most arch deed of piteous massacre
> That ever yet this Land was guilty of.
> Dighton and Forrest, who I did suborn
> To do this piece of ruthful butchery,
> Albeit they were fleshed villains, bloody dogs,
> Melting with tenderness, and mild compassion,
> Wept like to children, in their death's sad story.
> O thus (quoth Dighton) lay the gentle babes:
> Thus, thus (quoth Forrest) girdling one another
> Within their alablaster innocent arms:
> Their lips were four red roses on a stalk,
> And in their summer beauty kissed each other.
> A Book of Prayers on their pillow lay,
> Which once (quoth Forrest) almost chang'd my mind:

But O the Devil, there the villain stopped:
When Dighton thus told on, we smothered
The most replenished sweet work of Nature,
That from the prime Creation ere she framed.
Hence both are gone with conscience and remorse,
They could not speak, and so I left them both,
To bear this tidings to the bloody King.

There is a sense of strain in the passage. Lines are hammered out to fit the pattern of the metre —

'That éver yét this lánd was gúilty óf.'

Even the image of lips 'like four red roses on a stalk' was pretty rather than apt, deliberately sentimental. The whole description is written for effect and is without real feeling: it is painted passion.

Shakespeare's earliest style is quite distinguishable. His rhythms are regular; rhymes are common, used sometimes in alternate lines, more often in couplets. Occasionally he will even insert a sonnet into the dialogue. In the comedies there is much clever language, especially when young gentlemen are talking, which is sometimes tedious, for wit changes its fashion quickly. There is excessive outpouring of 'three-piled hyperboles' and imagery is often used for its own sake and not to clarify or intensify thought. In tragedy, and especially historical tragedy, Shakespeare was often bombastic and speeches were more heroic than suited the occasion. Shakespeare was still more interested in fine writing than in drama.

The best and the worst traits of his immature style are to be seen in the finest of his early plays, *Romeo and Juliet*.

Lady Capulet urges Juliet to fall in love with Count Paris in a speech which for twelve lines plays with the far-fetched conceit that Paris is a book:

> Read o'er the volume of young Paris' face,
> And find delight, writ there with beauty's pen,
> Examine every married lineament,
> And see how one another lends content:
> And what obscur'd in this fair volume lies,
> Find written in the margent of his eyes.
> This precious book of love, this unbound lover,
> To beautify him, only lacks a cover:
> The fish lives in the sea, and 'tis much pride
> For fair without, the fair within to hide:
> That book in many's eyes doth share the glory
> That in gold clasps locks in the golden story:
> So shall you share all that he doth possess,
> By having him, making yourself no less.

This is tediously clever.

Later Juliet, impatiently waiting for night and Romeo, breaks out into a lyric ecstasy which is just as elaborately poetical, but yet perfect:

> Gallop apace, you fiery-footed steeds,
> Towards Phoebus' lodging, such a waggoner
> As Phaethon would whip you to the west,
> And bring in cloudy night immediately.
> Spread thy close curtain love-performing night,
> That runaways eyes may wink, and Romeo
> Leap to these arms, untalk'd of and unseen,
> Lovers can see to do their amorous rites,
> By their own beauties, or if love be blind,
> It best agrees with night: come civil night,
> Thou sober-suited matron all in black,
> And learn me how to lose a winning match,

Play'd for a pair of stainless maidenhoods.
Hood my unmann'd blood baiting in my cheeks,
With thy black mantle, till strange love grow bold,
Think true love acted simple modesty:
Come night, come Romeo, come thou day in night,
For thou wilt lie upon the wings of night,
Whiter than new snow on a raven's back:
Come gentle night, come loving black-brow'd night,
Give me my Romeo, and when he shall die,
Take him and cut him out in little stars,
And he will make the face of heaven so fine,
That all the world will be in love with night,
And pay no worship to the garish Sun.
O I have bought the mansion of a love,
But not possess'd it, and though I am sold,
Not yet enjoy'd, so tedious is this day,
As is the night before some festival,
To an impatient child that hath new robes
And may not wear them.

The early style disappeared very rapidly as Shakespeare's experiences grew and with them his power of expression.

About two years later he wrote *The Merchant of Venice* (c. 1595). His serious dialogue was now better than his comic. Shylock expresses his hatred of Antonio plainly, clearly, and passionately, for Shakespeare had entered into Shylock's mind and had felt his emotion:

Signior Antonio, many a time and oft
In the Rialto you have rated me
About my moneys and my usances:
Still have I borne it with a patient shrug,
(For sufferance is the badge of all our Tribe).
You call me misbeliever, cut-throat dog,
And spet upon my Jewish gabardine,

And all for use of that which is mine own.
Well then, it now appears you need my help:
Go to then, you come to me, and you say,
Shylock, we would have moneys, you say so:
You that did void your rheum upon my beard,
And foot me as you spurn a stranger cur
Over your threshold, moneys is your suit.
What should I say to you? Should I not say,
Hath a dog money? Is it possible
A cur can lend three thousand ducats? or
Shall I bend low, and in a bondman's key
With bated breath, and whisp'ring humbleness,
Say this: Fair sir, you spet on me on Wednesday last;
You spurn'd me such a day; another time
You call'd me dog: and for these courtesies
I'll lend you thus much moneys.

There is still just a trace of stiffness in the rhythm, a slight but perceptible pause at the end of each line, but not a superfluous word or unnecessary metaphor. Even Portia's set speech on 'Mercy' in the Trial Scene is appropriate in the occasion and the expression.

In the first part of *Henry IV*, written perhaps nine months later, Shakespeare was first completely master of his medium. This play has a wide range of very different characters, each skilfully contrasted, but each speaks in a language which in phrase, structure, and rhythm is entirely appropriate. The most brilliant example of the contrast is in the scene where Hotspur, Glendower, Worcester, and Mortimer, compact their alliance. Shakespeare gained much by deliberate contrast. Hotspur, out of the ambition engendered in a hot head, cries out:

By heaven methinks it were an easy leap,
To pluck bright honour from the pale-fac'd moon,
Or dive into the bottom of the deep,
Where fadom-line could never touch the ground,
And pluck up drowned honour by the locks,
So he that doth redeem her thence might wear
Without corrival all her dignities,
But out upon this half-fac'd fellowship.

Falstaff, with the cynicism that comes from cold feet, grumbles:

'Tis not due yet, I would be loath to pay him before his day, what need I be so forward with him that calls not on me? Well, 'tis no matter, honour pricks me on; yea, but how if honour prick me off when I come on? how then? Can honour set to a leg? no, or an arm? no, or take away the grief of a wound? no. Honour hath no skill in surgery then? no. What is honour? a word. What is in that word honour? what is that honour? air. A trim reckoning. Who hath it? he that died a' Wednesday. Doth he feel it? no. Doth he hear it? no. 'Tis insensible then? yea, to the dead. But will it not live with the living? no. Why? detraction will not suffer it, therefore I'll none of it. Honour is a mere scutcheon, and so ends my catechism.

The contrast enhances both speakers and speeches.

Between *Henry IV* and *Hamlet* Shakespeare's technique developed rather than changed. There is not much in the dialogue or poetry of *Hamlet* that had not in some form appeared in earlier plays, but it is more competent, more supple. Each character, in long speeches or in conversation, not only speaks appropriately, but behind the words lies the whole compass of its particular personality and experience. This is seen in the less as well as the more im-

portant scenes. Thus, for instance, Hamlet having returned so dramatically to Denmark tells Horatio of his
adventure on the ship which was to take him to England
and to his destruction:

> Up from my cabin
> My sea-gown scarf'd about me in the dark,
> Grop'd I to find out them; had my desire,
> Finger'd their packet, and in fine, withdrew
> To mine own room again, making so bold,
> (My fears forgetting manners) to unseal
> Their grand commission, where I found Horatio,
> Oh royal knavery: an exact command,
> Larded with many several sorts of reasons;
> Importing Denmark's health, and England's too,
> With hoo, such bugs and goblins in my life,
> That on the supervise no leisure bated,
> No not to stay the grinding of the axe,
> My head should be struck off.

HORATIO: Is't possible?
HAMLET: Here's the commission, read it at more leisure:
But wilt thou hear me how I did proceed?
HORATIO: I beseech you.
HAMLET: Being thus be-netted round with villains,
Or I could make a prologue to my brains,
They had begun the play. I sate me down,
Devis'd a new commission, wrote it fair,
I once did hold it as our statists do,
A baseness to write fair; and labour'd much
How to forget that learning: but sir now,
It did me yeoman's service: wilt thou know
The effects of what I wrote?
HORATIO: Ay, good my lord.
HAMLET: An earnest conjuration from the King,
As England was his faithful tributary,
As love between them, as the palm should flourish,

> As Peace should still her wheaten garland wear,
> And stand a comma 'tween their amities,
> And many such-like As'es of great charge,
> That on the view and know of these contents,
> Without debatement further, more or less,
> He should the bearers put to sudden death,
> Not shriving-time allow'd.

In its place this speech is simply a piece of necessary information to explain how Hamlet came back. The description is vivid, but it is purely Hamlet's; and, moreover, it shows a little more of Hamlet's own personality and experience: his youthful lessons in handwriting, the touch of conscious snobbery, his sardonic relish of the flowery pomposities of formal correspondence, his ruthlessness when roused.

The power of expression can be seen at its best in some of the soliloquies in Hamlet. Soliloquy was an old device. In modern stage conditions it always appears artificial, but it was common and appropriate in the intimacy of the Elizabethan playhouses.

In his earlier plays Shakespeare used it mainly for two purposes: to give information, or as an excuse for the recitation of a reflective poem. Thus Richard III naïvely tells the audience that he is not indeed what he seems to others:

> I do the wrong, and first begin to brawl.
> The secret mischiefs that I set abroach,
> I lay unto the grievous charge of others.
> Clarence, whom I indeed have cast in darkness,
> I do beweep to many simple gulls;

Namely, to Derby, Hastings, Buckingham,
And tell them 'tis the Queen, and her allies,
That stir the King against the Duke my brother.
Now they believe it, and withal whet me
To be reveng'd on Rivers, Dorset, Grey;
But then I sigh, and, with a piece of Scripture,
Tell them that God bids us do good for evil:
And thus I clothe my naked villainy
With odd old ends, stolen forth of holy Writ,
And seem a Saint, when most I play the devil.

Thus Richard II, alone in his prison, soliloquizes leisurely on Life and Time in a poetical essay of sixty lines.

Hamlet also soliloquizes; in general reflection, as in his broodings over suicide – 'To be or not to be' – but more often in passages which reveal also the movements of his mind, his perplexities and resolutions. At times this revelation is so subtle that Shakespeare shows not only Hamlet's mind working, but even the subconscious thought beneath. After the play-scene Claudius has rushed away, unable to conceal his guilt any longer. He tries to pray. As he is kneeling, Hamlet passes by. He is keyed up for the murder that is to revenge his father. He sees the unwitting King. He feels that the supreme moment has come. He moves towards the King:

Now might I do it pat [*drawing his sword*], now he is praying,
And now I'll do't [*approaching the King*], and so he goes to Heaven,
And so am I reveng'd: [*he poises to thrust. The supreme moment has
        come. He is about to take his revenge: but the word 'Heaven'
        echoes. It is no vengeance to send Claudius to Heaven. The
        moment, after all, is not fitting. He lowers his point, and steps
        back.*] that would be scann'd,
A villain kills my father, and for that

I, his sole son, do this same villain send
To Heaven.

> [*He pauses the time of four stresses in silence as the thought takes root. There comes back to his mind the murder which was to be avenged, and the Ghost's story, with its bitterest complaint 'Cut off even in the blossoms of my sin, Unhousel'd, disappointed, unaneled. No reckoning made, but sent to my account With all my imperfections on my head.' Death, here and now, would be a benefit to Claudius*]

O this is hire and salary, not revenge.
He took my father grossly, full of bread,
With all his crimes broad blown, as flush as May,
And how his audit stands, who knows, save Heaven:
But in our circumstance and course of thought
'Tis heavy with him: and am I then reveng'd,
To take him in the purging of his soul,
When he is fit and season'd for his passage?
No.
Up sword, and know thou a more horrid hent
When he is drunk asleep: or in his rage,
Or in th'incestuous pleasure of his bed,
At gaming, swearing, or about some act
That has no relish of salvation in't,
Then trip him, that his heels may kick at Heaven,
And that his soul may be as damn'd and black
As Hell, whereto it goes. [*Then with a final swirl of passion as he strides off*] My mother stays,
This physic but prolongs thy sickly days.

Othello, written some months later, is perhaps the most perfectly constructed of all Shakespeare's plays, and may best be used to illustrate the four different kinds of speech which he uses: lyric poetry, rhyme, blank verse, prose. All are used in *Othello* with the greatest artistry and to gain particular effects of tone, mood, and atmosphere.

In Shakespeare's plays, and in Elizabethan drama generally, the broad distinction between the use of prose and the use of blank verse is clear and simple. Prose dialogue keeps the scene down to the ordinary level of every day. The characters talk to each other with an easy naturalism. Blank verse heightens the atmosphere, giving dignity and emotion to the speakers. Certain persons naturally speak verse, others prose. Falstaff naturally speaks in prose, Hotspur in verse, whilst Prince Hal speaks prose in the company of Falstaff and verse to his father.

In *Othello* blank verse is the natural speech of Othello himself. He is a heroic and dignified person. Iago, on the other hand, is a lower character altogether. He speaks mostly in prose, but at times he breaks into verse, especially in his soliloquies when he is left to himself. Other prose characters do not. When Benedick or Falstaff come to soliloquize they speak in their natural medium, prose. But there is a distinct purpose in every change in Iago's speeches. They coincide with and express the subtle changes of his mood. Iago, the jocular, simple 'honest Iago', speaks a quick prose. But Iago feigning honest indignation or expressing real hate is an emotional being; and verse, on the Elizabethan stage, is the natural expresson of emotion. At his first entry in the beginning of the play he is seething with anger because Othello has rejected him and chosen Cassio. This is the real Iago speaking from his heart. His hate jets out in spasms of indignant rhetoric:

> Despise me
> If I do not. Three Great-ones of the City
> (In personal suit to make me his Lieutenant)

Off-capp'd to him: and by the faith of man
I know my price, I am worth no worse a place.
But he (as loving his own pride, and purposes)
Evades them, with a bumbast circumstance,
Horribly stuff'd with epithets of war,
And in conclusion,
Nonsuits my mediators. For certes, says he,
I have already chose my officer. And what was he?
Forsooth, a great arithmetician,
One Michael Cassio, a Florentine,
(A fellow almost damn'd in a fair wife)
That never set a squadron in the field,
Nor the division of a battle knows
More than a spinster. Unless the bookish theoric:
Wherein the toged Consuls can propose
As masterly as he. Mere prattle (without practice)
Is all his soldiership. But he (Sir) had th'election;
And I (of whom his eyes had seen the proof
At Rhodes, at Cyprus, and on other grounds,
Christian, and heathen), must be be-leed, and calm'd
By debitor, and creditor. This counter-caster,
He (in good time) must his Lieutenant be,
And I (God bless the mark) his Moorship's Ancient.

It is not until Brabantio also loses his temper that Iago regains his self-control. Then once more he is outwardly the mocker, speaking prose. After further, but milder, expression of his anger he goes out. Next he appears in company with Othello. He is now feigning indignation, and verse is the proper medium for his speech.

In the scene in the Council Chamber Iago says nothing, but watches. At the end he is left alone with Roderigo. Again the mask is on and he speaks a flippant, supple prose until Roderigo leaves him. Then once more he is left alone and his real emotions break out in powerful passionate verse, as the idea of his plot begins to grow:

> How? How? Let's see.
> After some time, to abuse Othello's ears,
> That he is too familiar with his wife:
> He hath a person, and a smooth dispose
> To be suspected: fram'd to make women false.
> The Moor is of a free, and open nature,
> That thinks men honest, that but seem to be so,
> And will as tenderly be led by th'nose
> As asses are.

The rest of the line is silent, as the thought catches fire. Then with a little cry of triumph:

> I have't: it is engender'd: Hell, and Night,
> Must bring this monstrous birth, to the world's light.

Thus by watching the speech used by Iago we have a subtle revelation of his outward manner. With Iago prose shows that the mask is on, that he is self-controlled, 'honest' and frank. With Othello a lapse into prose denotes the opposite – a breakdown of control. Othello speaks prose only when he falls into his apoplectic fit and when he sees the handkerchief in Cassio's hand.

Another very good example of the different use of prose and verse occurs in the conversation between Desdemona and Emilia towards the end of the play. Othello has just gone out after his vile abuse of Desdemona. She suddenly asks:

> Dost thou in conscience think (tell me Emilia)
> That there be women do abuse their husbands
> In such gross kind?

EMILIA: There be some such, no question.
DESDEMONA: Wouldst thou do such a deed for all the world?
EMILIA: Why, would not you?
DESDEMONA: No, by this heavenly light.
EMILIA: Nor I neither, by this heavenly light:
       I might do't as well i' th' dark.
DESDEMONA: Wouldst thou do such a deed for all the world?
EMILIA: The world's a huge thing:
       It is a great price, for a small vice.
DESDEMONA: In troth, I think thou wouldst not.
EMILIA: In troth I think I should, and undo't when I had done.
       Marry, I would not do such a thing for a joint-ring,
       nor for measures of lawn, nor for gowns, petticoats,
       nor caps, nor any petty exhibition. But for all the
       whole world: 'uds pity, who would not make her
       husband a cuckold, to make him a monarch? I should
       venture Purgatory for't.

Emilia for the moment is confused by Desdemona's insistence and tries to turn it off in a laugh, but as Desdemona still persists she evades her by regaining her composure in indignant protestation – in rhetorical verse – against jealous husbands.

Shakespeare uses lyric verse to create a definite atmosphere. It is always sung. There are two notable examples in *Othello*. The first is in the drinking scene, where Iago sings:

And let me the canakin clink, clink:
And let me the canakin clink.
A soldier's a man: oh, man's life's but a span,
Why then let a soldier drink.
King Stephen was and a worthy peer,
His breeches cost him but a crown,
He held them sixpence all too dear,

With that he call'd the tailor lown:
He was a wight of high renown,
And thou art but of low degree:
'Tis pride that pulls the country down,
Then take thy auld cloak about thee.

Both songs are sung loudly and create the atmosphere of rowdy merriment which are the proper prelude and mood for Cassio's drunkenness.

The second is the Willow song. After the dreadful scene where Othello treats Desdemona as a prostitute Shakespeare wishes to prepare our mood for the murder. So Desdemona sings very softly:

The poor soul sat sighing, by a sycamore tree.
Sing all a green willow:
Her hand on her bosom, her head on her knee,
Sing willow, willow, willow.
The fresh streams ran by her, and murmur'd her moans,
Sing willow, willow, willow.
Her salt tears fell from her, and soften'd the stones,
Sing willow, willow, willow.
Sing all a green willow must be my garland.
Let nobody blame him, his scorn I approve.

I call'd my love false love: but what said he then?
Sing, willow, willow, willow.
If I court mo women, you'll couch with mo men.

The music has the same effect as a change of light in the modern theatre.

In *Othello* there is also a very notable instance of the use of rhyme. On the whole Shakespeare did not use much rhyme in his later plays. The rhymed couplet at the end of a scene was always liable to occur, but when he used rhyme within a scene it was with a definite purpose. In the Council Chamber scene, after Brabantio has been humiliated by Desdemona's unexpected declaration of her love for Othello, the Duke tries to comfort him by lapsing into proverbs, or 'sentences' as they were called:

> When remedies are past, the griefs are ended
> By seeing the worst, which late on hopes depended.
> To mourn a mischief that is past and gone,
> Is the next way to draw new mischief on.
> What cannot be preserv'd, when Fortune takes:
> Patience her injury a mock'ry makes.
> The robb'd that smiles, steals something from the thief,
> He robs himself, that spends a bootless grief.

Brabantio is irritated by these commonplaces, and retorts with a few proverbs of his own. Then, to point the contrast of mood, the Duke resumes not in blank verse, but in prose. Thus these two for the moment hold a kind of duet. As blank verse heightens speech and infuses it with emotion, so rhymed verse stiffens and gives it special emphasis. Here Shakespeare stressed the easy condolence of the man who was not touched by the sorrow of the inconsolable father. Then, as Brabantio goes out, he gives a parting message to Othello, which is both warning, prophecy, and curse:

> Look to her, Moor, if thou hast eyes to see:
> She has deceiv'd her father, and may thee.

The rhymed couplet gives just the touch of oracular pro-
nouncement necessary.

A few years later (1606) Shakespeare wrote *Lear* and
Macbeth. To those who are not familiar with Shakespeare's
language *Lear* is a difficult play to read because of its excessive concentration of thought. It is not so much that
he uses a strange vocabulary or difficult words, as that he
combines words and images to express thoughts which
are in themselves almost beyond expression. The play
itself was in some ways a new departure. He was concerned rather to show the significance of human conduct
than to tell a dramatic story. What he wished to say could
not be expressed in direct statement, but only by sugges-
tion and flashes of meaning. As in his earlier plays, he was
again consciously experimenting with language, but impatiently rather than joyously. He was no longer content
with blank verse. He wrote speeches in great sweeps and
not line by line, and even the formal pattern of five
stresses was submerged in the rush of the whole. Moreover the imagery was no longer simple or direct but ex-
ceedingly complex, suggesting a dozen different ideas and
associations in a sentence or two.

Edgar, disguised as the lunatic beggar, pauses in his
flight to reflect on his own wretched state:

> Yet better thus, and known to be contemn'd,
> Than still contemn'd and flatter'd, to be worst:
> The lowest and most dejected thing of Fortune,
> Stands still in esperance, lives not in fear:
> The lamentable change is from the best,
> The worst returns to laughter. Welcome then,

Thou unsubstantial air that I embrace:
The wretch that thou hast blown unto the worst,
Owes nothing to thy blasts.

[*He sees his father, now blinded and in agony, led by an old man.*]

But who comes here? My father poorly led?
World, world, O world!
But that thy strange mutations make us hate thee,
Life would not yield to age.

Macbeth, shrinking from the murder of Duncan, soliloquizes:

If it were done, when 'tis done, then 'twere well
It were done quickly: if th' assassination
Could trammel up the consequence, and catch
With his surcease, success: that but this blow
Might be the be-all, and the end-all. Here,
But here, upon this bank and school of time,
We'ld jump the life to come. But in these cases,
We still have judgement here, that we but teach
Bloody instructions, which being taught, return
To plague th' inventor. This even-handed Justice
Commends th' ingredients of our poison'd chalice
To our own lips. He's here in double trust;
First, as I am his kinsman, and his subject,
Strong both against the deed: then, as his host,
Who should against his murtherer shut the door,
Not bear the knife myself. Besides, this Duncan
Hath borne his faculties so meek; hath been
So clear in his great office, that his virtues
Will plead like angels, trumpet-tongu'd against
The deep damnation of his taking-off:
And Pity, like a naked new-born babe,
Striding the blast, or Heaven's cherubin, hors'd
Upon the sightless couriers of the air,

Shall blow the horrid deed in every eye,
That tears shall drown the wind. I have no spur
To prick the sides of my intent, but only
Vaulting Ambition, which o'erleaps itself,
And falls on th' other.

The imagery is too thickly clotted for paraphrase or analysis, but it expresses very adequately the turmoil of Macbeth's mind.

In *Lear* Shakespeare uses certain words and ideas in all their meanings and associations to be, as it were, the theme words of the story. They are *Nature* and *Nothing*. Lear, in his foolish optimism, regards the filial duty of affection as natural. When Cordelia offends him he casts her out as 'a wretch whom Nature is ashamed almost to acknowledge hers'. Later, when Goneril offends him, he curses her, calling on Nature to suspend her purpose: either to make Goneril childless, or, if she must have a child, that it may be 'a thwart disnatured torment to her'. Goneril and Regan he regards as 'unnatural hags', but in the end Cordelia 'redeems Nature from the general curse' that should follow her sisters' evil deeds.

Edmund the Bastard, the 'natural' son of Gloucester, begotten 'in the lusty stealth of Nature', dedicates himself to her:

Thou Nature art my Goddess, to thy Law
My services are bound.

for Nature is the Goddess of ruthless selfishness. 'Loyal and natural boy,' Gloucester calls him, with grim unconscious irony. Shakespeare uses 'nature', 'natural', 'naturally', forty-seven times in *Lear*. The words become a sinister echo throughout the play.

The word 'nothing' likewise is terribly significant. Cordelia, when her turn comes to praise her father and so justify his favouritism, is tongue-tied and can utter only 'Nothing, my Lord'.

'Nothing?' echoes Lear.

'Nothing.'

'Nothing will come of nothing, speak again.'

Lear is wrong, for from this 'nothing' comes everything. The word echoes in the parallel story of Gloucester, also mistaking the loyalty of his children.

'What paper were you reading?' he asks, as Edmund ostentatiously conceals the false letter which is to ruin Edgar.

He too replies, 'Nothing, my Lord,' and again from 'nothing' follows everything.

Antony and Cleopatra, if the accepted date (1607) is correct, followed *Lear* by some months. It lacks the vastness of *Lear*. Shakespeare was not consciously experimenting with this new technique of verse, but he had learnt much: he had developed new muscles. The theme did not allow for the titanic treatment of *Lear*, but the story, as Plutarch told it, called up in him an enthusiasm which he certainly did not feel in *Julius Caesar*, to which *Antony and Cleopara* was the sequel.

In the verse of *Antony and Cleopatra* there is a kind of resonance which he achieved nowhere else: it has a deep beauty quite its own. This quality comes out again and again in some haunting phrase or echo which exists in the sound of the words themselves, quite apart from their context:

> Oh, my oblivion is a very Antony,
> And I am all forgotten.

The exact meaning does not matter: it is a lovely sound in itself.

But poetry does not live by sound alone: it needs also perfect aptness of meaning. The finest example in the play is the description of Antony's first meeting with Cleopatra, which Shakespeare, with superb instinct, put into the mouth of cynic Enobarbus, when his friends at Rome are trying to get from him the latest Cleopatra scandal. Here Shakespeare reverted to a piece of sheer description of a kind that he had not allowed himself for years. His imagination was obviously kindled to write it by the gorgeous original in North's *Plutarch*, which was in itself a rich piece of prose. He held up the play that Enobarbus might describe the event, and in such a way that it might explain what was otherwise inexplicable, Cleopatra's power of fascinating Antony.

> I will tell you.
> The barge she sat in, like a burnish'd Throne
> Burnt on the water: the poop was beaten gold,
> Purple the sails: and so perfumed that
> The winds were love-sick.
> With them the oars were silver,
> Which to the tune of flutes kept stroke, and made
> The water which they beat, to follow faster;
> As amorous of their strokes. For her own person,
> It beggar'd all description, she did lie

In her pavilion, cloth-of-gold, of tissue,
O'er-picturing that Venus, where we see
The fancy outwork Nature. On each side her,
Stood pretty dimpled boys, like smiling Cupids,
With divers-colour'd fans whose wind did seem,
To glow the delicate cheeks which they did cool,
And what they undid did . . .

Her gentlewomen, like the Nereides,
So many mermaids tended her i' th' eyes,
And made their bends adornings. At the helm,
A seeming mermaid steers: the silken tackle,
Swell with the touches of those flower-soft hands,
That yarely frame the office. From the barge
A strange invisible perfume hits the sense
Of the adjacent wharfs. The city cast
Her people out upon her: and Antony
Enthron'd i' the market-place, did sit alone,
Whistling to th' air: which but for vacancy,
Had gone to gaze on Cleopatra too,
And made a gap in Nature . . .

Upon her landing, Antony sent to her,
Invited her to supper: she replied,
It should be better, he became her guest:
Which she entreated, our courteous Antony,
Whom ne'er the word of no woman heard speak,
Being barber'd ten times o'er, goes to the feast;
And for his ordinary, pays his heart,
For what his eyes eat only. . . .
I saw her once
Hop forty paces through the public street,
And having lost her breath, she spoke, and panted,
That she did make defect, perfection,
And breathless power breathe forth.
MAECENAS: Now Antony must leave her utterly.

ENOBARBUS: Never he will not:
    Age cannot wither her, nor custom stale
    Her infinite variety: other women cloy
    The appetites they feed, but she makes hungry,
    Where most she satisfies. For vilest things
    Become themselves in her, that the holy Priests
    Bless her, when she is riggish.

Apart from the sheer magnificence of the speech, it was not a mere bravery – Shakespeare showing off his powers as in the Queen Mab speech in *Romeo and Juliet* or Berowne's speech in *Love's Labour's Lost*. Nor was it only an orchestral setting for Cleopatra. It is, in anticipation, part of the music of Cleopatra's death; and it comes back at the end as an echo:

    Show me my women like a Queen: go fetch
    My best attires. I am again for Cydnus,
    To meet Mark Antony.

In death as in life

    Age cannot wither her, nor custom stale
    Her infinite variety.

And indeed the poetry of the play is full of echoes:

    Let Rome in Tiber melt, and the wide arch
    Of the rang'd Empire fall: here is my space,
    Kingdoms are clay: our dungy earth alike
    Feeds beast as man; the nobleness of life
    Is to do thus: when such a mutual pair,
    And such a twain can do't, in which I bind
    On pain of punishment, the world to weet
    We stand up peerless.

Thus Antony in his moment of triumphant love. And the echo comes back later from Cleopatra, alone and deserted, —

> My desolation does begin to make
> A better life: 'tis paltry to be Caesar:
> Not being Fortune, he's but Fortune's knave,
> A minister of her will: and it is great
> To do that thing that ends all other deeds,
> Which shackles accidents, and blots up change;
> Which sleeps, and never palates more the dung,
> The beggar's nurse, and Caesar's.

And again, Antony nearing his end:

> Unarm Eros, the long day's task is done,
> And we must sleep.

This is echoed by Iras to Cleopatra:

> Finish, good Lady, the bright day is done,
> And we are for the dark.

It is an echo and a contrast. To Antony, the long day meant work, and then rest: to Cleopatra brilliance. She must shine or go out.

There is another note in the incomparable music of this play: its changes of mood, tone, and pace. As a modern producer gains effects of change and contrast by lighting and music, so Shakespeare changed the atmosphere of his scenes by contrasts of verse, tone, and speed. In Act IV, Scene xii, there is a scene of battle. Antony is defeated. He enters raging against Cleopatra. She comes to him. He drives her away with fury and cursing. She reappears for a moment and runs off terrified by his wrath. And then, the fury exhausted and the passion spent, Antony returns with his servant Eros.

ANTONY: Eros, thou yet behold'st me?
EROS: Ay noble Lord.
ANTONY: Sometime we see a cloud that's dragonish,
          A vapour sometime, like a bear, or lion,
          A tower'd citadel, a pendent rock,
          A forked mountain, or blue promontory
          With trees upon't, that nod unto the world,
          And mock our eyes with air.
          Thou hast seen these signs,
          They are black Vesper's pageants.
EROS: Ay my Lord.
ANTONY: That which is now a horse, even with a thought
          The rack dislimns, and makes it indistinct
          As water is in water.

Antony, like the swan, is dying to slow music:

          So it must be, for now
     All length is torture: since the torch is out,
     Lie down and stray no farther. Now all labour
     Mars what it does: yea, very force entangles
     Itself with strength: seal then and all is done.

Between *Coriolanus* (c. 1607–8) and *Cymbeline* (c. 1610) there was apparently a period when Shakespeare wrote little. Then in 1610 and 1611 he wrote *Cymbeline*, *The Winter's Tale*, and *The Tempest*. *Cymbeline*, as a plot and a story, is a considerable decline from the level of a few years previously. *The Winter's Tale*, in its dialogue, is Shakespeare at his best, though the structure of the play, awkwardly broken by an interval of sixteen years between

Acts III and IV, is unequal. In *The Tempest* he achieved what some competent critics regard as his final and greatest play. In its poetry Shakespeare reached the farthest limits possible to the English language in expression and solemn music. The thought is still packed, but no longer obscure, the verse free but perfectly controlled. The English language, unlike Latin, is not suited for precise utterance: it has too many little monosyllables which are necessary to modify its meanings. A Roman could express in a single word every mood and tense of love by conjugating '*amo*'. An Englishman must add his 'I would' or 'I might have been'. Shakespeare in *The Tempest* showed what could be done, even with English.

In the later speeches he reached his final mastery over words. The meaning is clear, the thought deep, the emotional music perfect:

> You do look, my son, in a mov'd sort,
> As if you were dismay'd: be cheerful sir,
> Our revels now are ended: these our actors
> (As I foretold you) were all spirits, and
> Are melted into air, into thin air,
> And like the baseless fabric of this vision
> The cloud-capp'd Towers, the gorgeous Palaces,
> The solemn Temples, the great Globe itself,
> Yea, all which it inherit, shall dissolve,
> And like this insubstantial pageant faded
> Leave not a rack behind: we are such stuff
> As dreams are made on; and our little life
> Is rounded with a sleep: sir, I am vex'd,
> Bear with my weakness, my old brain is troubled:
> Be not disturb'd with my infirmity,
> If you be pleas'd, retire into my cell,

And there repose: a turn or two, I'll walk
To still my beating mind.

There will doubtless come a time when this prophecy
is fulfilled; but until the English language in its turn has
perished, in *The Tempest* lies its greatest achievement.

CHAPTER VIII

Editing Shakespeare

WHEN Shakespeare died in 1616 only fourteen of his plays were regularly in print, namely: *Richard III*, *Titus Andronicus*, *Love's Labour's Lost*, *Romeo and Juliet*, *A Midsummer Night's Dream*, *Richard II*, *Merchant of Venice*, *Henry IV* (Part I), *Henry IV* (Part II), *Much Ado About Nothing*, *Troilus and Cressida*, *Hamlet*, *Lear*, *Pericles*. *Othello* was printed in 1622, and pirated Quartos of *Romeo and Juliet*, *Henry V*, *Merry Wives of Windsor* and *Hamlet* had also appeared. The rest of his plays were first printed in 1623, when his surviving friends produced a collection in one volume known as the First Folio: it included also all the plays already printed, with the exception of *Pericles*.

In all Shakespeare's texts there are difficulties of reading and interpretation due to errors in printing. Sometimes the misprints are obvious; sometimes phrases and sentences are quite unintelligible. To make the text smooth and readable some tidying is necessary, particularly as Shakespeare apparently did not prepare his plays for printing. They were originally intended as scripts for actors and not as texts for readers. Scholars have therefore edited the texts, that is, have made alterations and additions to the originals with the intention of making them more intelligible and easy for the reader.

Until about forty years ago the original texts, Quarto or Folio, were not highly regarded. Editors believed that

Elizabethan printers were careless, ignorant men, who knew little of the refinements of literature, and could never be relied on to reproduce accurately the copy before them. Hence an edited text was preferable to an original.

Modern scholars, as the result of the exact study of Elizabethan texts, have established certain principles.

The most important authority for any text must be the author's own manuscript. No play manuscript used by a printer during Shakespeare's lifetime has survived.

The next most important text must be that printed directly from the manuscript. The earliest surviving text is therefore the most reliable, unless either a later text is based on a better original, or a later edition was revised by the author.

This sometimes happened with Shakespeare's plays. The first edition of *Hamlet* was a very bad pirated Quarto which came out in 1603; the second Quarto, dated 1604, was probably printed from Shakespeare's own manuscript, and is thus the better text.

When a play is constantly reprinted and changes of reading occur in later editions they are usually due to later editing and therefore of little value.

Elizabethan printing was not so haphazard as was formerly supposed; rather it differed in principle from modern usage and especially in matters of spelling, use of capitals and italic, and punctuation.

Even now, although English spelling is largely fixed, there are considerable minor differences in practice between the various printing and publishing houses. One firm, for instance, refuses to allow its authors to use an 's' in *civilization* or at the end of *northward*. Few authors who write in English are really expert in spelling, punctuation, or even the exact niceties of grammar, as they soon learn when a professional proof-reader has gone over their manuscript.

The history of the Elizabethan stage-play from the time when its author first sharpened his quill till it reaches a modern reprint is often very complicated; and particularly in the early part of Shakespeare's career, when as yet neither actors nor dramatists regarded plays as literature. Henslowe's *Diary*, especially between the years 1598 and 1602, gives the most valuable information. At this time Henslowe was acting as a banker to the players and made payments on their behalf to playwrights. These payments show how plays were written.

Most of the plays acted at his theatres were put together by syndicates of two, three, and sometimes even five writers. Playwriting was thus a practical business rather than high art. In 1598, for instance, Henry Chettle collaborated in the writing of twelve plays and made alterations in three others. In 1599 Thomas Dekker wrote two plays by himself and collaborated in fourteen. It may be worth noting that of the 280 plays mentioned by Henslowe about one in seven survives, and these are mostly the work of a single author. It was only natural that an author should be more interested in his own work and so take steps to have it printed; and that the creation of a single mind should be of greater artistic value.

The *Diary* also shows that popular plays were often revised with alterations and additions. Thus Marlowe's

Tragedy of Dr Faustus, one of the most popular Elizabethan plays, was first written in 1592. Henslowe recorded twenty-five performances between September 1594 and October 1597. It was entered for publication on 7 January 1601. Bird and Rowley, two of Henslowe's hacks, were paid for making additions to the play on 22 November 1602. The earliest surviving quarto of the play (which is presumably not the first edition, and is probably a pirated text), is dated 1604. A fourth quarto dated 1616 has considerable alterations and additions; and in a ninth quarto of 1663 there are still further changes.

Revision and collaboration are thus present in many Elizabethan plays, and as soon as Shakespeare's plays are closely examined, it is clear that they too have sometimes been altered and revised. Collaboration in a printed play can be detected only by style, and editors are seldom agreed on matters of style. There is, however, fairly general agreement that portions of *Macbeth*, particularly the Bloody Sergeant's Speech in Act i, Scene ii, and the Hecate scenes in Act iii, Scene v, and Act iv, Scene i, are not by Shakespeare. Collaboration would also explain the unevenness in *King John*.

Revision is obvious in the early texts of *Hamlet*, *Romeo and Juliet*, and *Love's Labour's Lost*. In the Second Quarto of *Hamlet* there are 218 lines which do not appear in the Folio and in the Folio 85 lines which do not appear in the Quarto. In the early Quartos of *Love's Labour's Lost* and of *Romeo and Juliet* there are instances where both the original and the revised version of a speech are printed. In the Second Quarto of *Romeo and Juliet* (1599) the last lines of

Romeo's final speech, Act v, Scene iii, are printed thus:

> Ah deare *Iuliet*
> Why art thou yet so faire? I will beleeue,
> Shall I beleeue that vnsubstantiall death is amorous,
> And that the leane abhorred monster keepes
> Thee here in darke to be his parramour?
> For feare of that I still will staie with thee,
> And neuer from this pallat of dym night
> Depart againe, come lye thou in my arme,
> Heer's to thy health, where ere thou tumblest in.
> O true Appothecarie!
> Thy drugs are quicke. Thus with a kisse I die.
> Depart againe, here, here, will I remaine,
> With wormes that are thy Chamber-maides: O here
> Will I set vp my euerlasting rest:
> And shake the yoke of inauspicious starres,
> From this world wearied flesh, eyes looke your last:
> Armes take your last embrace: And lips, O you
> The doores of breath, ſeale with a righteous kisse
> A dateless bargaine to ingrossing death:
> Come bitter conduct, come vnsauoury guide,
> Thou desperate Pilot, now at once run on
> The dashing Rocks, thy seasick weary barke:
> Heeres to my Loue. O true Appothecary:
> Thy drugs are quicke. Thus with a kisse I die.

In modern texts the lines repeated have been omitted. It is clear that Shakespeare rewrote and expanded the speech; but the printer misunderstood his copy and printed both the old and new ending.

It follows that every play must be carefully examined by itself to see whether there are any signs of its history. In general the history of a play manuscript is this. The author (or authors) having written the play delivered the manuscript to the company. The prompter then read it over and prepared it for performance by adding the necessary notes of the stage business and the like. The individual actors' parts were copied out with the cues. Amongst the Dulwich papers there still survives Alleyn's part as Orlando in Greene's *Orlando Furioso*. The play manuscript was then sent to the Master of Revels to be censored and licensed. The play was rehearsed and acted, and the manuscript was used in the theatre as a prompt-copy. When the play had passed out of the repertory the manuscript might be sold to a printer.

In many instances the text which reached the printer was the author's original manuscript. Towards the end of Shakespeare's career, however, when literary gentlemen liked to possess plays in their libraries, play manuscripts were copied out by professional copyists. There were good reasons for keeping the number of copies as low as possible, because as yet there was no dramatic copyright. The manuscript of a popular play might thus have been constantly altered and revised before it reached the printer, passages for omission being marked or scored through, and new additions being pasted or pinned in. It was easy for confusion and errors to arise.

All these processes can be illustrated from one of the few manuscripts of an Elizabethan stage-play which still exist. The manuscript is in the British Museum and is known as *The Book of Sir Thomas More*. It is a chronicle play of the usual type, showing scenes in the life and death of More. The manuscript is written in seven different handwritings; it has been revised and enlarged but apparently was never printed or played. Most of the play is in the handwriting of Antony Munday, but there are additions in other handwritings which have been labelled Hands A, B, C, D, and E. Of these, Hand E is Thomas Dekker's, and Hand C the Playhouse Reviser's of the Rose Theatre.

The manuscript also bears the observations and orders of Edmund Tilney, Master of the Revels, who censored it heavily because of the political significance of some of the speeches in the crowd and riot scenes. He sent the manuscript back with the note 'leave out the insurrection wholly and begin with Sir Thomas More at the Mayor's sessions with a report afterwards of his good service done, as Shreve of London upon a mutiny against the Lombards, only by a short report and not otherwise at your perils.'

Such a manuscript is in itself of great interest, but the more so since Hand D, which contributed three autographed pages in a scene showing Sir Thomas More haranguing a crowd of riotous citizens, is believed to be Shakespeare's. The case was argued at length in *Shakespeare's Hand and Sir Thomas More*, edited by A. W. Pollard.

The evidence is of three kinds: handwriting, spelling, and poetry.

The evidence from the handwriting is the least conclusive. Very little of Shakespeare's handwriting remains. Apart from some disputable specimens, only six undoubted signatures survive and the words *By me*. There is nothing remarkable in this lack of Shakespeare's autographs. Nothing at all survives of Greene's or Marlowe's writing, and of all the manuscripts used by Elizabethan printers during Shakespeare's lifetime there only survives one half of one. From handwriting alone it is not possible to say definitely whether Shakespeare did or did not write the Three Pages, which, however, are not in the known handwriting of any other dramatist.

The evidence from spelling is stronger. In the good Quartos of Shakespeare's plays, which were probably set up from his own manuscript, certain unusual spellings occur. The Elizabethan compositor was free and easy with spelling, but already a conventional spelling was beginning and certain spellings are rare in printed books. The printer would usually normalize an unconventional spelling; he would not make usual spelling abnormal. It is likely, therefore, that the curious spellings in the Quartos derive from Shakespeare's own manuscript. In the Three Pages certain letters are carelessly made and easily misread, especially *d* and *e* (which in Elizabethan handwriting are similar though of different size), and the 'minim' letters – *u* (which was also used for *v*), *m*, *n*, *i* (also used for *j*). Many of the misprints in the Quartos were due to confusion in the 'minim' letters; thus *five*, written *fiue*, could easily be misread as *fine* or *find*. The argument from spelling, though striking, is not conclusive because as yet no-one has undertaken a large and comprehensive study of Elizabethan spelling in general.

The literary evidence is the strongest. The crowd scenes in *Sir Thomas More* can be paralleled closely with other crowd scenes in Shakespeare's own plays: the Jack Cade scenes in *Henry VI*, the forum scene in *Julius Caesar*, and

the crowd scenes in *Coriolanus*. The speech itself is similar
in sentiment and rhythm to the great speech of Ulysses on
degree in *Troilus and Cressida*. The principal speech in the
Three Pages reads in a modernized version:

> Nay, certainly you are;
> For to the King God hath His office lent
> Of dread, of justice, power and command,
> Hath bid him rule, and will'd you to obey;
> And, to add ampler majesty to this,
> He hath not only lent the King His figure,
> His throne and sword, but given him His own Name,
> Calls him a god on earth. What do you, then,
> Rising 'gainst him that God Himself installs,
> But rise 'gainst God? What do you to your souls
> In doing this? O desperate as you are,
> Wash your foul minds with tears, and those same hands,
> That you like rebels lift against the peace,
> Lift up for peace, and your unreverent knees,
> Make them your feet to kneel to be forgiven!
> Tell me but this: what rebel captain,
> As mutinies are incident, by his name
> Can still the rout? Who will obey a traitor?
> Or how can well that proclamation sound,
> When there is no addition but a rebel
> To qualify a rebel? You'll put down strangers,
> Kill them, cut their throats, possess their houses,
> And lead the majesty of law in liom,
> To slip him like a hound. Say now th' king
> (As he is clement, if the offender mourn)
> Should so much come too short of your great trespass
> As but to banish you, whither would you go?
> What country, by the nature of your error,
> Should give you harbour? Go you to France or Flanders,
> To any German province, Spain or Portugal,
> Nay, anywhere that not adheres to England, —

Why, you must needs be strangers; would you be pleased
To find a nation of such barbarous temper,
That, breaking out in hideous violence,
Would not afford you an abode on earth,
Whet their detested knives against your throats,
Spurn you like dogs, and like as if that God
Owed not nor made not you, nor that the elements
Were not all appropriate to your comforts,
But chartered unto them, what would you think
To be thus used? This is the strangers' case;
And this your momtanish inhumanity.

In the manuscript, the speech is spelt and punctuated
thus:

Nay certainly you ar
for to the king god hath his offyc lent
of dread of iustyce, power and comaund
hath bid him rule, and willd you to obay
and to add ampler maiestie to this
he hath not only lent the king his figure
his throne and sword, but gyven him his owne name
calls him a god on earth, what do you then
rysing gainst him that god himsealf enstalls
but ryse gainst god, what do you to your sowles
in doing this o desperat as you are.
wash your foule mynds with teares and those same hands
that you lyke rebells lyft against the peace
lift vp for peace, and your vnreuerent knees
make them your feet to kneele to be forgyven;
tell me but this what rebell captaine
as mutynes ar incident, by his name
can still the rout who will obay a traytor
or howe can well that proclamation sounde
when ther is no adicion but a rebell
to quallyfy a rebell, youle put downe straingers

kill them cutt their throts possesse their howses
and leade the maiestie of law in liom
to slipp him lyke a hound; say nowe the king
as he is clement, yf thoffendor moorne
shoold so much com to short of your great trespas
as but to banysh you, whether woold you go.
what country by the nature of your error
shoold gyve you harber go you to France or Flanders
to any Iarman province, Spane or Portigall
nay any where that not adheres to Ingland
why you must needs be straingers, woold you be pleasd
to find a nation of such barbarous temper
that breaking out in hiddious violence
woold not afoord you, an abode on earth
whett their detested knyves against your throtes
spurne you lyke doggs, and lyke as yf that god
owed not nor made not you, nor that the elaments
wer not all appropriat to your comforts.
but charterd vnto them, what woold you thinck
to be thus vsd, this is the straingers case
and this your momtanish inhumanyty.

The case is not yet finally proved, as there are several
flaws in the original argument. The authors of *Shakespeare's
Hand* assigned the play to the year 1594 or thereabouts;
but Shakespeare could not have written the passage so
early, for he did not develop so competent and fluent a
style until at least five years later. A good case has, however, been made for the year 1601. If so, the passages
which so disturbed Edmund Tilney were sentiments which
might have been taken to refer to the rebellion of the
Earl of Essex, and the style is consistent with other plays
which Shakespeare wrote at this time.

The study of this manuscript has led to the founding of

a new principle of textual criticism: that when an editor proposes to emend a text which he suspects to be corrupt, he must take into account the author's handwriting. If his proposed emendation is not due to a probable misreading, then it is to be suspected. This is the principle adopted by Professor Dover Wilson in the *New Shakespeare*, which is sometimes called 'scientific bibliography'.

Actually, it is neither so scientific nor so infallible as it sounds. The modern editor has not seen the original manuscript; he can only guess what its appearance might have been. Even if it were possible to guess what the printer saw before him in his copy, the editor must also guess what the printer knew. Most men who write fast and not too legibly produce in their manuscripts words which are not in themselves clear; but the reader, knowing something of the matter in hand, can guess the meaning from the context. In a private letter there is usually not much difficulty. When, however, a manuscript is passed to a printer who knows little of the subject and is not particularly interested by it, he will guess the illegible words; and his guess will depend on his education and experience. Anyone who has had to deal considerably with printers and typists will have experienced this. The ignorant typist, unable to read her copy, will cheerfully produce nonsense; the second-class typist will not be content with nonsense, but will make a sense of her own. The perfect secretary will make a correct copy because she is familiar with the matter.

My own experience of printers (which is now considerable) has shaken my first faith in scientific bibliography.

The most striking instance occurred in a short introduction for an edition of Marston's *Malcontent*. Contrary to usual (and wiser) practice, a manuscript copy was sent to the printer. The proof returned with twenty-four errors in 2000 words — an unusually large proportion. Some of these errors were so striking that at first glance it seemed a telling confirmation of the value of 'scientific bibliography', but on comparing the proof with the original manuscript it worked the other way. Of the twenty-four errors only ten were due to misreading of the handwriting. For some the printer could not be held responsible: *Maeilente* for *Macilente*, *Lampateo* for *Lampatho*; *servants* for *seruants*. Others were possible misreadings of the script but made no sense in their context, as *make* for *unable*, *that* for *but*, *pave* for *grave*. The remainder were the printer's own unaided effort, such as *folies* for *follies*, *devision*, *reconizable*, *Johnson* for *Jonson* (twice), *John* for *Ihon* (in a quoted title page), *Parles Churchyard* for *Paul's Churchyard*. Three were particularly striking. I was made to speak of a character called *Tharsicles* in a play of *Troilus and Creosida*, and, most interesting of all, 'they [Marston's satires] pilloried many recognizable contemporaries' became (the printer's mind having strayed from Marston to a motor-cycle for two) they 'pillioned'. Of the twenty-four errors, less than half were due to the copy.

These errors were a revelation of the printer's mind and standard of education. Obviously he was bored with the matter and never gave a thought either to context or meaning. Nor was he used to literary copy. Had he known even the names of Shakespeare's plays he would have associated *Troilus* rather with *Cressida* than with *creosote;* he would have known that Ben's surname was spelt without an *h*.

The handwriting of an author is only one of many causes of error in the printed text, for at times printers will make the oddest mistakes even when following printed copy. In the Penguin Shakespeares, for instance, Bully Bottom appeared in one reprint as 'Billy', and 'incontinency' was watered down to 'inconsistency'. Elsewhere 'Queen Elizabeth' in printed copy re-appeared as 'Queer Elizabeth'. There is indeed no accounting for a large proportion of human errors.*

As has been seen, only a small proportion of Elizabethan plays was ever published; most of them have perished. The players objected to the publication of plays for practical reasons, but as the standard improved, so there grew up a literary interest in plays. It set the fashion amongst literary-minded gentlemen to read plays and to collect them in their libraries. Lord Mountjoy's secretary noted one of his recreations as reading play-books. Sir John Harington in 1610 possessed 129 play-books, and during the years 1600–10 he bought 90 out of 105 which were published during those years.† It became also a practice for certain authors to make a second copy of their plays

---

*Amongst other misprints which have come my way, the following is worth note. In a book on the Earl of Essex I wrote ' "*Well*," *sighed Essex*, "*it may be so*." ' The printer inexplicably produced ' "*Gos*," *sighed Essex*, "*it may be so*." ' Hereupon the proof-reader wrote in the margin: '*Query:* "*Gosh*"?'

†*Elizabethan Stage*, iii, p. 183.

and sell it to the printers, though this was considered hardly honest.

Sometimes play manuscripts were stolen, or if a play was particularly popular or topical some hack would be paid to vamp up a pirated copy. The pirated texts of *Henry V*, *Hamlet*, and *The Merry Wives of Windsor* were produced in this way. Sometimes when the players were hard up they sold their play-books. After the dislocation caused by the plague of 1592–4, twenty-two plays were published in one year. When a play had ceased to be profitable, it was sometimes sold; and there were occasions when for some particular reason it was desirable to allow printed copies to be circulated. Thus the Lord Chamberlain's Men allowed the first part of *Henry IV* to be published, probably to demonstrate to the world that Oldcastle's name had been changed to Falstaff.*

Although the players had no dramatic copyright in their plays, they were not without some protection. There was a printer's copyright; a printer, by the rules of the Stationers' Company, was obliged to enter the titles of books which he printed in the Stationers' Register. This gave him sole right to print. In practice, however, printers were very casual in observing the regulations, and only about two-thirds of the books printed were actually entered. Books were not allowed to be entered unless the authority of the wardens of the Stationers' Company, or of the Archbishop of Canterbury or the Bishop of London or the Privy Council, had first been secured. Players were sometimes able to prevent the unwarranted printing of

See p. 75.

their plays by appealing to their patrons. Sometimes they arranged with a printer to enter the play in the Stationers' Register and so secure copyright, but with no intention of printing it.

Elizabethan play-texts were often carelessly printed. Some authors, such as Ben Jonson, who had a high opinion of their own works, carefully supervised the printing, but most plays show little sign of editing or preparation for the press. The spelling is more erratic than in most Elizabethan books; there are no place-headings at the beginnings of scenes; the scenes are seldom marked, and often there is even no division into Acts. The punctuation is dramatic rather than grammatical. In the Quartos the punctuation is usually much lighter than in the Folio, and it is always worth careful note. Play manuscripts were punctuated to show how the speech should be pronounced, but in most of the Folio texts it has been very carefully revised.

It is surprising how varying texts can differ from each other in small particulars. The simplest way of following this is to set alongside the same passage as it occurs in succeeding versions. The passage chosen is from the last Act of *Hamlet*, when Hamlet and Laertes begin the fencing match. The texts are: A, the Second Quarto of 1604; B, the First Folio of 1623; C, Nathaniel Rowe's edition of 1709; D, the standard Globe edition first published in 1864; E, the new Cambridge *Shakespeare*, 1934.

A

King. Set me the ftoopes of wine vpon that table,
If *Hamlet* giue the firft or fecond hit,
Or quit in anfwere of the third exchange,
Let all the battlements their ordnance fire.
The King fhall drinke to *Hamlets* better breath,
And in the cup an Vnice fhall he throwe,
Richer then that which foure fucceffiue Kings
In Denmarkes Crowne haue worne: giue me the cups,
And let the kettle to the trumpet fpeake,
The trumpet to the Cannoneere without,
The Cannons to the heauens, the heauen to earth.
Now the King drinkes to *Hamlet*, come beginne.　*Trumpets*
And you the Iudges beare a wary eye.　　　　　　*the while.*
　　Ham. Come on fir.
　　Laer. Come my Lord.
　　Ham. One.
　　Laer. No.
　　Ham. Iudgement.
　　Ostrick. A hit, a very palpable hit.　*Drum, trumpets and fhot.*
　　Laer. Well, againe.　　　　　*Florifh, a peece goes off.*
　　King. Stay, giue me drinke, *Hamlet* this pearle is thine.
Heeres to thy health: giue him the cup.
　　Ham. Ile plays this bout firft, fet it by a while
Come, another hit.　　　What fay you?
　　Laer. I doe confeft.
　　King. Our fonne fhall winne.
　　Quee. Hee's fat and fcant of breath.
Heere *Hamlet* take my napkin rub thy browes,
The Queene carowfes to thy fortune *Hamlet*.
　　Ham. Good Madam.
　　King. Gertrard doe not drinke.
　　Quee. I will my Lord, I pray you pardon me.
　　King. It is the poyfned cup, it is too late.

From the Second Quarto of 1604. This text was probably set
up from Shakespeare's own manuscript. Note the spellings
'Vnice', 'Cannoneere', 'Ostrick', 'Gertrard', 'poysned'.

B

King. Set me the Stopes of wine vpon that Table:
If *Hamlet* giue the firſt, or ſecond hit,
Or quit in anſwer of the third exchange,
Let all the Battlements their Ordinance fire,
The King ſhal drinke to *Hamlets* better breath,
And in the Cup an vnion ſhal he throw
Richer then that, which foure ſucceſſiue Kings
In Denmarkes Crowne haue worne.
Giue me the Cups,
And let the Kettle to the Trumpets ſpeake,
And Trumpet to the Cannoneer without,
The Cannons to the Heauens, the Heauen to Earth,
Now the King drinkes to *Hamlet*. Come begin,
And you the Iudges beare a-wary eye.
   Ham. Come on ſir.
   Laer. Come on ſir.   *They play.*
   Ham. One.
   Laer. No.
   Ham. Iudgement.
   Oſr. A hit, a very palpable hit.
   Laer. Well: againe.
   King. Stay, giue me drinke.
Hamlet, this Pearle is thine,
Here's to thy health. Giue him the cup,
               Trumpets ſound, and ſhot goes off.
   Ham. Ile play this bout firſt, ſet by a-while.
Come: Another hit; what ſay you?
   Laer. A touch, a touch, I do conſeſſe.
   King. Our Sonne ſhall win.
   Qu. He's fat, and ſcant of breath.
Heere's a Napkin, rub thy browes,
The Queene Carowſes to thy fortune, *Hamlet*.
   Ham. Good Madam.
   King. *Gertrude*, do not drinke.
   Qu. I will my Lord;
I pray you pardon me.
   King. It is the poyſon'd Cup, it is too late.
From the First Folio text of 1623, probably set up from a play-
house manuscript. Note the minor differences.

C

King. Set me the Stopes of Wine upon that Table:
If *Hamlet* give the firſt, or ſecond hit,
Or quit in anſwer of a third exchange,
Let all the Battlements their Ordnance fire.
The King ſhall drink to *Hamlet's* better breath,
And in the Cup an Union ſhall he throw
Richer than that, which four ſucceſſive Kings
In *Denmark's* Crown have worn. Give me the Cups,
And let the Kettle to the Trumpets ſpeak,
The Trumpets to the Canoneer without,
The Canons to the Heav'ns, the Heav'n to Earth,
Now the King drinks to *Hamlet*. Come, begin,
And you the Judges bear a wary Eye.

   Ham. Come on, Sir.
   Laer. Come on, Sir.   *[They play.*
   Ham. One.
   Laer. No.
   Ham. Judgment.
   Oſr. A hit, a very palpable hit.
   Laer. Well—— again——
   King. Stay, give me drink. *Hamlet*, this Pearl is thine,
Here's to thy health. Give him the Cup.
               [Trumpet ſound, Shot goes off.
   Ham. I'll play this bout firſt, ſet it by a while.
Come——another hit——what ſay you? *[They Play again.*
   Laer. A touch, a touch, I do confeſs.
   King. Our Son ſhall win.
   Queen. He's fat, and ſcant of breath.
Here's a Napkin, rub thy brows,
The Queen carouſes to thy fortune, *Hamlet*.
   Ham. Good Madam ——
   King. *Gertrude*, do not drink.
   Queen. I will, my lord; I pray you pardon me.
   King. It is the poiſon'd Cup, it is too late.   *[Aſide.*

From Nathaniel Rowe's edition of 1709. Note the regularized
text and stage directions, and the revised punctuation.

D

King. Set me the stoups of wine upon that table.
If Hamlet give the first or second hit,
Or quit in answer of the third exchange,
Let all the battlements their ordnance fire;
The king shall drink to Hamlet's better breath;
And in the cup an union shall he throw,
Richer than that which four successive kings
In Denmark's crown have worn. Give me the cups;
And let the kettle to the trumpet speak,
The trumpet to the cannoneer without,
The cannons to the heavens, the heavens to earth,
'Now the king drinks to Hamlet!' Come, begin:
And you, the judges, bear a wary eye.

 Ham. Come on, sir,
 Laer.   Come, my lord. [*They play.*
 Ham.   One.
 Laer.   No.
 Ham.   Judgment.
 Osr. A hit, a very palpable hit.
 Laer.   Well; again.
 King. Stay; give me drink. Hamlet, this
  pearl is thine;
Here's to thy health.

   [*Trumpets sound ; and cannon shot off within.*
      Give him the cup.
 Ham. I'll play this bout first; set it by awhile.
Come. [*They play.*] Another hit; what say you?
 Laer. A touch, a touch, I do confess.
 King. Our son shall win.
 Queen.   He's fat, and scant of breath.
Here, Hamlet, take my napkin, rub thy brows;
The queen carouses to thy fortune, Hamlet.
 Ham. Good madam!
 King.   Gertrude, do not drink.
 Queen. I will, my lord; I pray you, pardon me.
 King. [*Aside.*] It is the poison'd cup: it is
  too late.

From the Globe *Shakespeare* (first published in 1864). This is
the form most familiar to most modern readers.

E

King. Set me the stoups of wine upon that table.
If Hamlet give the first or second hit,
Or quit in answer of the third exchange,
Let all the battlements their ordnance fire.
The king shall drink to Hamlet's better breath,
And in the cup an union shall he throw,
Richer than that which four successive kings
In Denmark's crown have worn; give me the cups,
And let the kettle to the trumpet speak,
The trumpet to the cannoneer without,
The cannons to the heavens, the heaven to earth,
'Now the king drinks to Hamlet.' Come, begin,
And you, the judges, bear a wary eye.

    (*the cups are set at his side ; trumpets sound ;*
      Hamlet and Laertes take their stations)

Hamlet. Come on, sir.
Laertes.   Come, my lord.
      They play
Hamlet.   One!
Laertes.   No.
Hamlet.   Judgment?
Osric. A hit, a very palpable hit.
  [*they break off ; the kettle-drum sounds, the trumpets*
  blow, and a cannon-shot is heard without
Laertes.   Well, again.
King. Stay, give me drink. [*a servant fills a cup*]
  Hamlet, [*he holds up a jewel*], this pearl is thine.
Here's to thy health! [*he drinks and then seems to cast*
       the pearl into the cup
   Give him the cup.
Hamlet. I'll play this bout first, set it by a while.
    [*the servant sets it on a table behind him*
Come.
     They play again
  Another hit! What say you?
Laertes. A touch, a touch, I do confess't.
       [*they break off.*
King. Our son shall win.
Queen.   He's fat, and scant of breath.

Here, Hamlet, take my napkin, rub thy brows.
> [*she gives it him, and going to the table*
> *takes up his cup of wine*

The queen carouses to thy fortune, Hamlet.
 Hamlet. Good madam!
 King.   Gertrude, do not drink.
 Queen. I will, my lord, I pray you pardon me.
> [*she drinks and offers the cup to Hamlet*

 King. It is the poisoned cup, it is too late!

From *The New Shakespeare*, edited by J. Dover Wilson. The latest method of editing Shakespeare.

A modern editor is thus faced with many new problems, especially in producing an edition intended for the general reader. There is so much interest in the recent work of scholars that the older 'authorized version' is no longer suitable. For the student an exact facsimile of the Quarto or Folio is the most valuable text. But the general reader is troubled by the old tall *s* which so closely resembles an *f*, and can lead to awkward mistakes, or the use of *u* for *v*, *i* for *j*, and other Elizabethan practices such as *yᵉ* for *the* or *yᵐ* for *them*. An editor must compromise both in printing and in arrangement.

In the Penguin Shakespeares the text follows the original very closely. The place-headings which were added to the beginnings of scenes by editors of the eighteenth century have been abandoned. Act and scene divisions are marked only for reference. Stage directions follow the original as closely as possible. The old punctuation has been kept unless it seems obviously impossible.

Such principles seem simple until an editor tries to carry them out. Even when there is only one original text – the Folio – there are difficult problems. In *Macbeth*, for instance, the Folio text sometimes prints short lines of verse. Editors have often joined them to make complete blank-verse lines, rearranging the rest of the speech. Shakespeare sometimes began a blank-verse speech with a half-line. This irritates editors, who shift the lines up to make them look better, until they come to some line which cannot be moved. Then they leave it as a broken line and start again.

When, however, a Folio text is closely studied it is clear that much of *Macbeth* is not written in formal blank verse at all, but in a free, rhythmic verse; so also is *Antony and Cleopatra* and *Coriolanus*. But readers and even critics have not realized that Shakespeare often wrote in a free verse, because they are not accustomed to use the Folio.

For an instance. After the murder of Duncan, Lady Macbeth and her husband are surprised by the knocking; she tries to bring him to his senses. In the authorized text the speech appears:

> My hands are of your colour, but I shame
> To wear a heart so white.—[*Knocking within.*] I hear a knocking
> At the south entry: retire we to our chamber:
> A little water clears us of this deed:
> How easy it is, then! Your constancy
> Hath left you unattended. [*Knocking within.*] Hark! more
>   knocking.
> Get on your night-gown, lest occasion call us,
> And show us to be watchers. Be not lost
> So poorly in your thoughts.

The quick, jerky utterance is much more effectively shown in the Folio printing:

My Hands are of your colour: but I shame
To weare a Heart so white.   *Knocke.*
I heare a knocking at the South entry:
Retyre we to our Chamber:
A little Water cleares us of this deed.
How easie is it then? your Constancie
Hath left you unattended.   *Knocke.*
Hearke, more knocking.
Get on your Night-Gowne, least occasion call us,
And show us to be Watchers: be not lost
So poorely in your thoughts.

The editor's worst difficulties come when there are
two or more early texts: a Quarto and a Folio. In some
instances the printer of the Folio used a printed Quarto
and made little alteration.

One of the most difficult texts is *King Lear*. There are
about five hundred differences of reading between the
Quarto and Folio. The Folio text, as a close examination
shows, was set up from a copy of the Quarto most carefully corrected. Presumably, therefore, the Folio gives
what its editors regarded as the best version. Sometimes,
however, the Quarto is better than the Folio and often
entirely different. Hitherto editors have simply followed
one another, choosing their readings at haphazard from
either text, and not always the better reading.

There is a good example in the opening scene. When
Lear turns to Cordelia to give her judgement, according
to the Quarto version he says:

                         but now our joy,
Although the last, not least in our deere love,
What can you say to win a third, more opulent
Than your sisters?

In the Folio the version is:

> Now our Joy,
> Although our last and least; to whose young love,
> The Vines of France, and Milk of Burgundie,
> Strive to be interest. What can you say, to draw
> A third, more opulent than your Sisters? speak.

Editors choose the Quarto reading, arguing, presumably, that Shakespeare would have chosen the common, proverbial phrase 'last but not least'. Thereby they miss the whole point of the speech. Cordelia was presented as a little creature, physically overshadowed by Goneril and Regan. Lear cannot understand how so small a body should seemingly contain so brazen a heart.

When such problems occur, as they do frequently, an editor can only follow his own judgement. In general he should be guided by principles, but he soon finds that he cannot follow them consistently. He can only comfort himself with the bleak thought that he will have the same reward or punishment as all others who write or edit books. If his work pleases, it will succeed; if not it will disappear. Editing Shakespeare is, indeed, more of an art than a science.

A SHORT READING LIST

I. GENERAL

A Companion to Shakespeare Studies. Edited by Harley Granville-Barker
and G. B. Harrison. 1934.
   An Introduction to the various branches of modern Shakespeare
   study, each chapter being written by an expert.

Shakespeare's England : An Account of the Life and Manners of his Age.
Edited by Sir Walter Raleigh. 2 vols. 1916.
   A series of studies, each written by an expert, of the many
   activities and branches of life in Shakespeare's England.

William Shakespeare : A Study of Facts and Problems. By Sir E. K.
Chambers. 2 vols. 1930.
   Though hardly suitable for general reading, this is an indispensable
   reference book for the serious student.

The Elizabethan Journals : 1592–1603. By G. B. Harrison. 3 vols. in one.
1928–33.

A Jacobean Journal: 1603–6. By G. B. Harrison. 1941.
   A day-to-day account of those things most talked of during these
   years.

II. THE THEATRE

The Elizabethan Theatre. By Sir E. K. Chambers. 4 vols. 1923.
   An indispensable book for students.

Henslowe's Diary. 2 vols.

Henslowe's Papers. Edited by W. W. Greg. 1904–8.
   The most important and interesting collection of original documents covering the Elizabethan playhouse.

The Globe Playhouse. By John C. Adams. 1942.
   The best account of the playhouse.

Shakespeare's Audience. By Alfred Harbage. 1941.
   A valuable study of the people for whom Shakespeare wrote.

A Short Reading List

III. THE SHAKESPEARE TEXT

Mr William Shakespeares Comedies, Histories, & Tragedies. Edited by Helge Kökeritz and C. T. Prouty, 1954.
  A facsimile, reduced in size, of the famous First Folio photographically reproduced and convenient for general reading.

Shakespeare's Fight with the Pirates. By A. W. Pollard. 1919.
  Mainly responsible for the modern interest in textual study.

Shakespeare's Hand in 'Sir Thomas Moore'. By A. W. Pollard and others. 1923.
  An examination of the reasons for believing that three pages of this manuscript play are in Shakespeare's autograph.

The Editorial Problem in Shakespeare. By W. W. Greg. 1942.

The Cambridge Shakespeare. Edited by W. G. Clark and W. A. Wright. 9 vols. 1863–6.
  This edition and its more popular version, the *Globe Shakespeare*, (first published in 1864) was long, and by many still is, regarded as the 'authorized version' of Shakespeare.

The New Variorum Shakespeare. Begun by H. H. Furness in 1871 and still in progress.
  Each volume contains a summary and large extracts of the most important work on each play.

The New Shakespeare. Edited by Sir Arthur Quiller-Couch and J. Dover Wilson. 1921.
  This text is the result of modern textual theories. The first – *The Tempest* – contains a general introduction setting out the principles which the editors originally intended to follow.

IV. CRITICISM

Shakespeare Criticism. (From the beginnings to Carlyle.) Edited by D. Nichol Smith. 1916.
Shakespeare Criticism 1919–35. Edited by Anne Bradby. 1936.
  Two useful collections of representative specimens.

Shakespeare. By Sir Walter Raleigh. 1907.
  Although over fifty years old, still one of the best of the general studies of Shakespeare.

A Short Reading List

Selections from the Shakespearian criticism of S. T. Coleridge and William Hazlitt will be found in the Everyman Library.

Shakspere: A critical study of his mind and his art. By Edward Dowden. 1875.
One of the most important and sanest of Victorian critics.

Shakespearian Tragedy. By A. C. Bradley. 1904.
The most elaborate critical study of the four great tragedies.

Shakespeare's Workmanship. By Sir A. T. Quiller-Couch. 1918.
A lively demonstration that Shakespeare was a man of the theatre.

Prefaces to Shakespeare. By Harley Granville-Barker. 1923–46.
  I. *Love's Labour's Lost. Julius Caesar. King Lear.*
  II. *Romeo and Juliet. The Merchant of Venice. Antony and Cleopatra.*
  III. *Hamlet.*
  IV. *Othello.*
The most important critical examination of these plays – from the point of view of the producer and student of the stage – that has yet appeared.

Shakespeare's Problem Comedies. By W. W. Lawrence. 1931.
Most valuable for the less read plays.

Shakespeare's Imagery and What It Tells Us. By Caroline F. E. Spurgeon. 1935.
The first and in many ways still the most important work on this aspect of Shakespearian criticism.

The Wheel of Fire. By G. Wilson Knight. 1930.
This work together with *The Imperial Theme* and *The Crown of Life* are subjective and imaginative interpretations of the ideas suggested by Shakespeare's imagery.

The Great Stage. By R. B. Heilman. 1948.
An elaborate study of the imagery of *King Lear* and a good example of the latest kind of study of Shakespeare's poetic processes.

Shakespeare's World of Images: the development of his moral ideas. By Donald Stauffer. 1949.
A mid twentieth-century version of what Dowden attempted in 1875.

A Short Reading List

V. REFERENCE

The most generally useful bibliography is the section given to Shakespeare in *The Cambridge Bibliography of English Literature* by F. W. Bateson, 1940. Later work is recorded in the more important periodicals, especially *The Shakespeare Survey*, an annual survey of Shakespearian study and production, edited by Allardyce Nicoll, and *Shakespeare Quarterly*, American Shakespeare Association of New York.

A New and Complete Concordance to Shakespeare. By John Bartlett. 1906.

The Shakespeare Allusion Book. By J. J. Munro. 1931.

A Shakespeare Glossary. By C. T. Onions. 1911.